Scientific Names of
Southern African Birds Explained

Scientific Names of Southern African Birds Explained

Is it all Greek to you?

Antonios Andreanidis

authorHOUSE®

AuthorHouse™ UK
1663 Liberty Drive
Bloomington, IN 47403 USA
www.authorhouse.co.uk
Phone: 0800.197.4150

Published by AuthorHouse 09/16/2016

ISBN: 978-1-5246-3613-5 (sc)
ISBN: 978-1-5246-3614-2 (e)

cover photo taken by the author at HwangeNP, Zimbabwe

Print information available on the last page.

HOW TO READ THIS BOOK

The names of the persons who identified and/or named the bird and the year they did so are mentioned at the end of each name.

The family name of the bird and its common name can be found in brackets.

The two numbers after the common name of the bird are page numbers of the two books where you can find more information about the bird. The SASOL Complete Photographic field guide, Birds of Southern Africa, 2009 and Robert's Birds of Southern Africa, 2009.

Where there is only one number then it is the family name of the bird and that is the page of Robert's Birds of Southern Africa, 2009.

Where there is a Greek word it is also written in Greek so readers interested in researching further can do so in Greek dictionaries or other books. Some bird names are from other languages (Arabic, Indian etc). Where I managed to find their original spelling I wrote it down.

When more than one birds have the same name I list all of them with their family names and the names of the people who named them.

ACKNOWLEDGEMENTS

Any book that is about scientific names of any form of life must start and pay tribute to the father of modern taxonomy **Carl Linnaeus**, the Swedish botanist, physician and zoologist who was determined to name all life.

Two books I used and were invaluable to writing this book were Beolens' and Watkins' 2003 'Whose bird' of 2003 and J. A. Jobling's Dictionary of scientific Bird names of 2010.

The first is a wonderful book about the people after who some birds were named.

The second is the epitome of scientific work in the field of scientific names of birds of the whole world. I was in awe when I got it in my hands. I only hope my book adds a little something to Mr. Jobling's Herculean task. Both books are also used as references by Wikipedia.

Last but not least the amazing Dictionary of Ancient Greek by Lydell & Scott was a tremendous help.

A

abdimii after the Turkish (of Albanian origin) governor of Dongola in Sudan, Bey El- Arnaut *Abdim* or Abidin Bey (1780-1827); he was a commander and politician during the early years of Muhammad Ali's rule; he helped Rüppel on his North African expedition (*ciconia*, abdim's stork also white-bellied stork, 70, 621) M. Lichtenstein, 1823.

aberrans L. deviant, aberrant; *aberrare*, to deviate, to stray, to wander, to escape; *ab + erro* be wrong, make a mistake; Eng. error; Fr. erreur; Ita. errore; related to Gr. *erro* (ἔρρω) move slowly, be lost, be ruined (*cisticola*, lazy cisticola, 336, 826) A. Smith, 1843.

abingoni after Montagu Bertie Lord Norreys of Rycote, the 5th Earl of *Abingdon* (1784-1854), Lord-Lieutenant of Berkshire, who may have been a member of A. Smith's expedition in Africa in 1834 (*campethera*, golden-tailed woodpecker, 258, 131) A. Smith, 1836.

abyssinica Abyssinia is the old name of Ethiopia but in ornithology it also includes Eritrea; the origin of the word is the arabic *habesh* which means 'a mixture of many nations' related to the amharic word *hbsh*, 'mixed'; some peoples in the region are still called Habesha (*hirundo*, lesser striped swallow, 276, 756) F. E. Guérin-Méneville, 1843.

accipiter L. hawk; metaphorically thief, grabber, marauder; *accipiter, -tris* from latin *accipere*: to grasp, take, accept, let in, learn (40)

achaetops Gr. like *chaetops*; L. *ad* to, towards, near; khaite (χαίτη) long flowing hair or mane; *opsis* (ὄψις) face; it means it has hair on the face like the rock-jumpers (chaetops), referring to presence of eyelashes (50).

acridotheres Gr. *locust hunter*; *akrida* (ἀκρίς, ἀκρίδος) locust or grasshopper; *thera* (θήρα) *hunting wild animals; therao* (θηράω) to hunt wild animals; the Greek word for hunting is also in the scientific names of lion, leopard etc (pan-*thera*) and the common name of pan-ther; it means 'hunter of everything' (55).

acrocephalus Gr. edge of head; *akron* (ἄκρον) edge akros (ἄκρος) is what is at the edge, highest; pointed is not one of the meanings of the word and acrobatic adds a word that is simply not there; cephale (κεφαλή ancient Greek and κεφάλι modern Greek) head; acro-bat, acro-nym, acro-polis; cephalo-pod, en-cephal-itis (51).

actitis Gr. coast dweller; akti (ἀκτή) coast, shore, beach (36).

actophilornis Gr. shore or beach loving bird; akti (ἀκτή) coast, shore, beach; filos (φίλος) friend or lover; ornis (ὄρνις) bird; the word for bird was both male and female in ancient Gr.; in modern Gr. it is female and it means chicken (36)

acunhae after the most remote inhabited archipelago in the world and the main island of the same archipelago, Tristan da Cunha (Tristan d'Acunha), which is the anglicised name of Tristão da Cunha, the Portuguese explorer who first sighted the islands in 1506. They lie in the South Atlantic and are part of the British overseas territory of St Helena, Ascension and Tristan da Cunha (nesospiza, inaccessible bunting or inaccessible island finch, 414) J. Cabanis, 1873.

acuta /acutus L. sharp pointed; acutus sharp-pointed, keen, severe, intelligent; acuere sharpen; refers to sharp pointed tail (anas, northern pintail, 84, 113) C. Linnaeus, 1758.

acuticaudus L. sharp-pointed tail; acutus sharp-pointed, keen, severe, intelligent; cauda tail (lamprotornis, sharp-tailed starling, 368, 965) J. V. Barboza du Bocage, 1870.

adansonii after Michel Adanson (1727-1806) French naturalist, botanist and collector in Senegal 1748-1753; the generic name of the baobab (adansonia digitata) commemorates Adanson as well (coturnix, blue quail, 132, 78) (Verreaux & Verreaux 1851)

adeliae after Adelie Dumont d'Urville (1798-1842), wife of Admiral Jules-Sebastian-Cesar Dumont d'Urville who first found this penguin; the Adelie coast of Antarctica is also named after her; the Admiral is the one who convinced the French to acquire the statue of Venus of Milo, now in the Louvre (pygoscelis, adelie penguin, 18) J. B. Hombron & H. Jacquinot, 1841.

adsimilis L. like, similar; adsimilis like; dicrurus named by Johann

Matthäus Bechstein in 1794; the name either refers to uniformly black plumage (Roberts, 2009) or Bechstein (1794) thought the Drongo to have the form of the Jackdaw *Coloeus* (Dicrurus) (Jobling, 2010, pp32) (dicrurus, fork-tailed drongo, 284, 684).

adspersus L. sprinkling; a*spergere* to sprinkle referring to the black spotted wings and mantle or scattered, not in flocks; *ad+spargo* from Gr. *spargao* (σπαργάω) to be full (pternistis, red-billed spurfowl, 126, 70) G. R. Waterhouse, 1838.

adusta L. brown or burnt; *adustus* burnt, scorched, dusky, dark; *adurere* to burn (muscicapa, african dusky flycatcher, 340, 920) H. Boie, 1828.

aegypius Gr. vulture; *aegypios* (αἰγυπιός) vulture; the difference to *gyps* being that *aegypios* snatched living animals (40).

aegyptiaca Gr. of Egypt; from Accadian Hut-ka-ptah 'temple of the soul of Phthah', an egyptian deity, originally referring to Memphis; Aegyptus was the king of Egypt who fathered 50 sons and 49 of them were murdered by the 49 daughters of his twin brother Danaus; in Ancient Egyptian the land was called *kemet* 'black country'; today in Arabic it is called *Misr* مصر (alopochen, egyptian goose, 78, 91) C. Linnaeus, 1766.

aegyptius Gr. Egyptian (milvus, yellow-billed kite, 112, 479) J.F.Gmelin 1788.

aenigmatolimnas Gr. puzzling pools or lakes; *aenigma,- atos (αἴνιγμα, -ατος)* a riddle, mystery, puzzle; *limne (λίμνη)* lake, pool (35).

aequatorialis L. equatorial; *aequus* equal, flat (tachymarptis, mottled swift, 228, 236) J. W. von Müller, 1851.

aequinoctialis L. equinoctial; a*equus* equal, flat; *nox, noctis* night; referring to the stormy waters of the Cape of Good Hope, usually associated with the equinox and the nocturnal habits of the bird (procellaria, white-chinned petrel, 38, 668) C. Linnaeus 1758.

aereus L. of bronze or copper, referring to the colour of the plumage; *aes, aeris* bronze or copper (ceuthmochares, green malkoha, 218, 215) L.J.P. Vieillot, 1817.

aeruginosus L. rusty; *aerugo, -inis* rust or copper rust; metaphorically envy, greed, rapacity (circus, western marsh-harrier, 106, 500) C. Linnaeus 1758.

aethereus Gr. etherial; a*etherios (αἰθέριος)* high in the air, heavenly and also gracious referring to the bird's graceful flight; Eng. <u>ether</u> *(αἰθέρας)* was for Homer the layer above the atmosphere and for Plato and Aristotle the fifth element of Nature (phaethon, red-billed tropic bird, 50, 563) C. Linnaeus, 1758.

aethiopicus Gr. Ethiopian; *aetho (αἴθω)* to burn; *ops,-ops (ὄψ, ὀπός)* face; sunburnt face, which was the name for black people who lived south of the Nile (laniarius, tropical boubou, 360, 696, J. F. Gmelin, 1788) (threskiornis, african sacred ibis, 76, 611, J. Latham, 1790).

affinis L. neighbouring, associated with; *adfinis* neighbouring or associated with; in the case of the little swift Roberts suggests its habit to breed close to man; in the case of the flufftail Roberts again suggests that it refers to its similarity to existing taxa within crex (apus, little swift, 230, 240 J. E. Gray 1830) (sarothrura, striped flufftail, 140, 319, A. Smith, 1828).

afra/ afer/africana/ africanus L. african; *afra* is the female form of *afer* and they both mean African; it used to mean Lybia and generally Northern Africa, west of Egypt; it is not considered correct as originating from L. *aperio* 'to open (towards the sun), shed light' but rather connected to the Afri tribe that is maybe related to the semitic word *afar* for 'dust or soil' (actophilornis africanus, african jacana, 136, 382, J. F. Gmelin, 1789) (afrotis afra, southern black korhaan, 146, 298, C. Linnaeus, 1758) (afrotis afraoides, northern black korhaan, 146, 298, C. Linnaeus, 1758) (bubo africanus, spotted eagle-owl, 222, 257, C. J. Temminck 1821) (buphagus africanus, yellow-billed oxpecker, 370, 973, C. Linnaeus 1766) (cinnyris afer, greater double-collared sunbird, 376, 990, C. Linnaeus 1766) (euplectes afer, yellow-crowned bishop, 388, 1026, J. F. Gmelin 1789, the subspecies that occurs in the area is E. a. taha. Taha is either Old High German, where daw derives from or Tswana *thaga* for a small bird like a weaver (Jobling 2010, pp 378) (mirafra africana, rufous-naped lark, 264, 862, A. Smith, 1836) (nilaus afer, brubru, 364, 688, J. Latham, 1801) (parus afer, grey tit, 290, 742, J. F. Gmelin 1789) (gyps africanus, white-backed vulture, 86, 488, T. Salvadori, 1865) (rhinoptilus africanus, double-banded courser, 180, 421, C. J. Temminck, 1807) (phalacrocorax africanus, reed cormorant, 56, 572, J. F. Gmelin, 1789) (pternistis afer, red-necked spurfowl, 126, 73, P. L. S. Müller, 1766) (pytilia afra, orange-winged pytilia, 398, 1060, J. F. Gmelin, 1789) (scleroptila africanus, grey-winged frncolin, 130, 64, J. F. Stephens, 1819) (sphenoeacus afer, cape grassbird, 322, 781, J. F. Gmelin, 1789) (turtur afer, blue-spotted wood-dove 204, 288, C. Linnaeus, 1766) (upupa africana, african hoopoe, 248, 160, the subspecies of the area was named by J. M. Bechstein in 1811)

afraoides. as above with the Greek ending –oides added, which means resembling (afrotis, northern black korhaan, 146, 298) A. Smith, 1830.

africanoides like African; -*oides* is the Greek ending for resembling (calendulauda, fawn-coloured lark, 266, 870) A. Smith, 1836.

afrotis *afer* is from Latin and it means African; it was used by the Romans to refer to modern day Tunisia or Libya; Gr. *otis* (ὠτίς) bustard (34).

agapornis Gr. lovebird; *agape* (ἀγάπη) love; *ornis* (ὄρνις) bird in ancient Gr.; the word for bird was both male and female in ancient Gr.; in modern Gr. it is female and it means chicken; the name refers to the strong monogamous relationship of the bird (32)

aguimp Roberts claims it is French and it means with a wimple, referring to black hood on head, neck and sides of face; Jobling claims it is Namaqua and it means shore-runner (2009, pp 36) (motacilla, african Pied wagtail, 348, 1089) C.Dumont de Sainte-Croix, 1821.

alario L. on the wing; *alarius* on the wing (of an army), pertaining to the auxiliary cavalry i.e a flier; *ala* wing, ward, squadron, flank, army's wing; Eng. aisle, Fr. aile (serinus, black-headed canary, 410, 1117) C. Linnaeus, 1758.

alba/albus L. white, bright; *albus* white, bright, pale, fair, clear; from Gr. *alphos* (ἀλφός) sub-white leprocy of the face (calidris alba, sanderling, 162, 364, P. S. Pallas, 1764) (chionis alba, greater sheathbill, 178, 385, J. F. Gmelin 1789) (corvus albus, pied crow, 288, 723, P. L. Statius Müller, 1776) (egretta alba, great egret, 64, 585, C. Linnaeus, 1758) (platalea alba, 74, 612, G. A. Scopoli, 1786) (tyto alba, barn owl, 222, 251, G. A. Scopoli, 1769).

albescens L. whitish; *albescere* to become white, to dawn (calendulauda, karoo lark, 268, 872) F. de Lafresnaye, 1839.

albiceps L. white-headed; *albus* white, bright, pale, fair, clear; *-ceps* headed (*caput* head) (vanellus, white-crowned lapwing, 158, 411, J. Gould, 1834) (psalidoprocne, white-headed saw-wing, 280, 763, P. L. Sclater, 1864).

albicollis L. white-necked; *albus* white, bright, pale, fair, clear; *collum* neck (corvus, white-necked raven, 288, 724, J. Latham, 1790) (ficedula, collared flycatcher, 344, 923 C. J. Temminck, 1815) (merops, white-throated bee-eater, 240, 189 L. J. P. Vieillot, 1817).

albifrons L. white foreheaded; *albus* white or bright, pale, fair,

clear; *frons, frontis* forehead, brow or facade (amblyospiza, thick-billed weaver, 382, 1036, N. A. Vigors, 1831) (sterna, little tern, 194, 463, P. S. Pallas, 1764).

albigularis/albogularis L. white-throated; *albus* white, bright, pale, fair, clear; *gula* throat (crithagra albogularis, white-throated canary, 408, 1127, A. Smith, 1833) (hirundo albigularis, white-throated swallow, 278, 750, H.E. Strickland, 1849).

albiventris L. white-bellied; *albus* white, bright, pale, fair, clear; *venter, -ris* stomach, belly; Eng. *venter, ventr*iloquist (halcyon, brown-hooded kingfisher, 236, 181) G. A. Scopoli, 1786.

albofasciata L. white-banded; *albus* white, bright, pale, fair, clear; *fascia* band, bandage, streak of clouds; the name refers to the white tip of the tail (chersomanes, spike-heeled lark, 272, 878) F. de Lafresnaye, 1836.

albonotata/albonotatus L. white-marked; *albus* white, bright, pale, fair, clear; *nota,-ae* mark or sign from L. *nosco* to know, to learn from Gr. gnosco (γνώσκω) and *gignosco* *(γιγνώσκω)* to know (elminia, white-tailed crested-flycatcher, 342, R.B. Sharpe, 1891) (euplectes albonotatus, white-winged widowbird, 390, 1033 J. Cassin, 1848).

alboterminatus L. white-ended, white-edged; *albus* white, bright, pale, fair, clear; *terminare* to end, to limit (tockus, crowned hornbill, 246, 153) J. Büttikofer, 1889.

alcedo L. kingfisher; *alcedo* kingfisher; Gr. *alkyon (ἀλκυών)* kingfisher (30).

alcinus Jobling (2009, pp 40) offers *auk-like* as explanation, auk being a family of birds with their bills compared to that of the Black Bat Hawk; a subfamily of auk birds is called *Alcinae* and also the genus *Alca* named by Linnaeus in 1758; Roberts (2009, pp 477) claims it derives from Gr. and it means strong or brave; the Gr. word is *alkimos (ἄλκιμος)* and it does mean strong, brave (macheiramphus, bat hawk, 118, 477) C. L. Bonaparte, 1850.

alectoris Gr. the common hen *(ἀλεκτορίς);* male *alector (ἀλέκτωρ)* from *a+lektros (α+λέκτρος)* without a bed, without a wedding bed (26).

alexandrinus Gr. of Alexandria, Egypt; Alexander the Great, king of Macedonia and son of Philip the 2nd, built eighteen cities, first among them Alexandria in Egypt, and named them after himself; his name *Alexandros Ἀλέξανδρος* means 'he who defends men'; *alex andras*(charadrius, kentish plover, 154, 402) C. Linnaeus, 1758.

alleni after Rear-Admiral William *Allen* (1793-1864), an English naval officer who was involved in fighting the African slave trade; he led three expeditions to Africa; two in 1832 and one in 1841, to the Niger where he collected the type specimen at Idda (Beolens & Watkins, 2003, pp.24) (porphyrio, allen's gallinule, 136, 332) T. R. H. Thomson, 1842.

alopochen Gr. fox-goose; *alopeex (ἀλώπηξ)* fox; *chen, -os (χήν,- ός)* goose; there is no Greek language error as *alopo-* is a synthetic of many Greek adjectives; the name refers to the colour of the bird (27).

alpina L. alpine; *alpes* alps, high mountains; *albus* white referring to snow covered mountain tops (calidris, dunlin, 162, 372) C. Linnaeus, 1758.

amadina according to Jobling, it is the corrupt diminutive of ammodramus which in Greek means sand runner (ἄμμος sand; δραμεῖν is the past infinitive of *treho* (τρέχω) to run) (57).

amandava a genus of the estrildid finches; other names were used in the past like *amadavat, amaduvad* and *avidavad;* they are all corruptions of *Ahmedabad,* the largest city and former capital of the state of Gujarat, India.

amaurornis Gr. dark bird; *amauros* (ἀμαυρός) dark, dim; *ornis* (ὄρνις) bird (35).

amblyospiza Gr. blunt finch; *amvlys* ἀμβλύς blunt or dull; *spiza* σπίζα finch (57).

ameliae Jobling in 1991 (pp. 10) wrote that the bird was named after Marquise *Amélie* de Tarragon, wife of French explorer Marquis Léone de Tarragon, who visited South Africa in 1840-1841, and Roberts (pp. 1099) agrees but refers to de Tarragon as a nobleman and amateur ornithologist; Jobling in 2009 (pp. 44) mentions *Amélie* Goislard de Villebresme Marquise de Tarragon, mother (and not wife) of Léonce de

Tarragon Marquis de Tarragon (macronyx, rosy-throated longclaw, 356, 1099) de Tarragon, 1845.

amethystina Gr. amethyst-coloured; *amethystos* (ἀμέθυστος) may be translated as 'not drunk' as ancient Greeks believed that the semi-precious stone, the violet variety of quartz, protects people from drunkeness (chalcomitra, amethyst sunbird, 378, 981) G. Shaw, 1812.

ammomanopsis Gr. appearing like genus ammomanes; *ammomanes* (ἀμμομανής) passionately fond of sand; *ammos* (ἄμμος) sand; *manes* from *mania* (μανία) passionately fond; *opsis* (ὄψις) appearance or face (53).

amurensis from the Russian name of the tenth longest river in the world that forms part of the border between Siberia and China and where the bird breeds; Amur, Ru. Амур (falco, amur falcon, 122, 552) G. Radde, 1863.

anaethetus Gr. senseless; *anaesthetos,* (ἀναίσθητος) senseless, without perception; these birds were not afraid of man and were easy to catch or kill, like anous (onychoprion, bridled tern, 194, sterna, 466) G. A. Scopoli, 1786.

anaplectes Gr. from the ancient verb *anapleco* (ἀναπλέκω), to weave, to ornate, to wreath (57).

anas L. duck; *anas, -anatis* duck (27).

anastomus Gr. open; *anastomoo* (ἀναστομόω) to open; refers to the opening or gap that the openbill storks have in the middle part of their bills (44).

anchietae after José Alberto de Oliveira *Anchieta* (1832-1897), a 19th century Portuguese explorer, naturalist and collector who travelled mainly in Angola and probably Mozambique (antichromus, anchieta's tchagra, 360, 691) J. V. Barbosa du Bocage, 1869.

andropadus Gr. man's supporter; *aner, andros (ἀνήρ, ἀνδρός)* man; *opados (ὀπαδός)* supporter, attendant; (A. importunus was a nuisance because it followed hunters and alerted other birds and animals by constantly chattering) (50).

angolensis angolan; from *ngola*, the title held by the kings of Ndongo, powerful vassals to the kingdom of Kongo; the Portuguese named the area *reino de Angola* around 1571 (gypohierax, palm-nut vulture, 88, 483, J. F. Gmelin, 1788) (hirundo, angola swallow, 278, 749, J. V, Barbosa du Bocage, 1868) (monticola, miombo rock-thrush, 300, 900, Sousa, 1888) (uraeginthus, blue waxbill, 396, 1054, C. Linnaeus, 1758) (pitta, african pitta, 232, 677, L. J. P. Vieillot, 1816).

anguitimens L. Anguitenens is the latin name of the constellation of Ophiuchus, snake holder in Gr. (eurocephalus, southern white-crowned shrike, 364, 730) A. Smith, 1836.

angulata L. angular, cornered; *angulus* angle, corner; probably has to do with the pointed, frontal shield (gallinula, lesser moorhen, 134, 335) C. J. Sundevall, 1850.

anhinga Amazonian dialect (Tupi); it means little head, devil bird or snake bird or according to Roberts water turkey (42).

anomalospiza Gr. irregular finch; *anomalos (ἀνώμαλος)* out of the ordinary, ` unusual, irregular; *spiza (σπίζα)* finch (58).

anous Gr. stupid or mindless; privative α- and *nous (νοῦς)* the mind; these birds were not afraid of predators or hunters and were easy to catch (39).

antarctica Gr. opposite the bear; *anti (ἀντί)* opposite or against; arctos *(ἄρκτος)* bear; bear being the Northern constellations of Ursus Minor and Ursus Major (small bear and big bear); the brightest star of the former, Polaris is very close to the north celestial pole making it the northern pole star (for now). Zeus had a son with Callisto, Arkas, and his wife Hera turned Callisto into a bear. Years later the bear met her son, a young man by now and ran towards him. He was ready to kill the bear (his mother) but Zeus turned him into a young bear and to save them from Hera put them in the sky, where they are the constellations of big and small bears. Hera ordered Oceanus, who represented the sky, to never let those two set. That's why the two constellations are always visible from the northern hemisphere (catharacta, subantarctic skua, 182, 431, R. Lesson, 1831) (pygoscelis, chinstrap penguin, 18, 630, J. R. Forster, 1781) (thalasssoica, antarctic petrel, 32, 657, J. F. Gmelin, 1789).

anthobaphes Gr. flower coloured; *anthos (ἄνθος)* flower; *baphe (βαφή)* colour or paint (56).

anthoscopus Gr. flower examiner or watcher; *anthos (ἄνθος)* flower, blossom; *scopos (σκοπός)* he who watches, guard, searcher (49).

anthreptes Gr. flower feeder; *anthos (ἄνθος)* flower, blossom; *threptes (θρέπτης)* feeder comes from *threpsis (θρέψις)* nutrition (56).

anthropoides Gr. human-like; *anthropos (ἄνθρωπος)* human (hence the study of humans is anthropology in english);-*oides* resembling; according to some linguists *anthropos* actually means the creature that looks like a man, a male *(ἀνδρός, ὄψις)* (34).

anthus Gr. flower; *Anthus (Ἄνθος)* was a mythological figure that was devoured by horses and Zeus and Apollo turned him and his whole family into birds; Anthus became a bird that immitated the neighing of horses but fled at their sight; Anthus was also a bird mentioned by Pliny, probably the yellow wagtail (motacilla flava) (59).

antichromus Gr. different colour; *anti* (ἀντί) opposite, against; *chroma,-tos* (χρῶμα, -τος) colour (48).

apalis Gr. soft, tender; *apalos (ἀπαλός)* soft, tender, delicate (52).

apaloderma Gr. soft skin; *apalos (ἀπαλός)* soft; *derma (δέρμα)* skin; Eng. *derma*tologist is a skin doctor (29).

apiaster L. bee-eater; *apis* bee; Eng. *api*ary (merops, european bee-eater, 238, 194) C. Linnaeus, 1758.

apiata L. resembling parsley or celery; *apium* can be either celery or parsley (mirafra, cape clapper lark, 264, 865) L. J. P. Vieillot, 1816.

apivorus L. bee-eater; *apis* bee; *vora (βορά)* from ancient Greek means food, where the Latin verb *vorare* (to swallow or devour) comes from (pernis, european honey-buzzard, 104, 476) C. Linnaeus, 1758.

aplopelia Gr. simple or single dove; a*plos (ἀπλός)* simple; *pelia (πέλεια)* the stock dove (columba oenas) for its dusky colour; *peleia (πέλεια)* the wild pigeon

Columba oenas thus named because of its dark colour; *peleiai (πέλειαι)* priestesses that could foresee the future as did the magic pigeons of Dodoni; *pelios (πελιός)* bruised; *Pelias,* king of Iolkos, was named after the dark mark he had on his face, by a horse kick when he was deserted with his twin brother, *Neleas,* by their mother (33).

aptenodytes Gr. unfeathered or unwinged diver; privative α- without; *ptenon (πτηνόν)* having feathers or wings and later bird; *dytes (δύτης)* diver, from the verb *dyo* δύω) to dive or to plunge and is the same word Greeks use for the sun when it sets as from most of Greece the sun looks like it dives into the sea (44).

apus Gr. without feet or legs; privative α- without; *pus, podos (ποῦς, ποδός)* foot; these birds have small and weak legs (32).

aquila L. eagle; from *aquilus* swarthy, dark-coloured for Aquila chrysaetos, the golden eagle; the *aquila* was the most important symbol of the Roman legion and A. *chrysaetos* was the model for it; the soldier carrying the symbol was known as the *aquilifer* the eagle-bearer; Eng. *aquili*ne (40).

ardea L. a heron; Jobling reports the following beautiful muth; the city of Ardea, near ancient Rome, *was razed to the ground and* from the ashes rose a lean, pale bird, shaking the cinders from its wings and uttering mournful cries (Jobling, 2009, pp. 54) (42).

ardens L. glowing, burning, impassive, ardent; from verb *ardere* to be on fire, burn, shine; Roberts (2005, pp. 1034), claims the name comes from *inaccurate illustration which shows a red belly spot, described as 'like a glowing coal'* (euplectes, red-collared widowbird, 390, 1034) P. Boddaert, 1783.

ardeola L. small heron and generic name of the Squacco Heron and pond herons; bird looks like a plover and has the features of a heron (dromas, crab plover, 150, 419) G. von Paykull, 1805.

ardeotis L. &. Gr. heron bustard; *ardea* heron in L. and *otis, -idos* (ὠτίς, -ίδος) bustard in Gr. (34).

ardesiaca/ardosiaceus L. slate-coloured, slatey; French *ardoisé* slate, a fine-grained, foliated metamorphic rock (egretta ardesiaca, black heron, 66, 582 J. G. Wagler, 1827) (falco ardosiaceus, grey kestrel, 120, 548, L. J. P. Vieillot, 1823).

arenaria L. sand-loving or related to sand in reference to coastal habitat; *arena* sand; *arenaria* also means gladiator (36)

aridulus L. somewhat dry (Jobling, 2009, pp.55), of dry places or desert (Roberts, 2009, pp. 839); diminutive of *aridus* arid, dry from verb *arere* to be dry (cisticola, desert cisticola, 330, 839) H. F. Witherby, 1900.

ariel medieval folklore Ariel, a spirit or sylph of the air; it is a given name from Biblical Hebrew אריאל *Ariel* that literally means "lion of God" (fregata, lesser, 58, 628) G. R. Gray, 1845.

armatus L. armed; *arma, -orum* weapons, armour, shield; Roberts (2005) finds reference to carpal spurs of the bird (vanellus, blacksmith lapwing, 158, 408) W. J. Burchell, 1822

arnoti after David *Arnott* (1822-1894), who was a renowned, unscrupulous South African attorney; he lived at Colesberg, and contributed fossil reptiles, mammals, birds and insects to the South African Museum between 1858 and 1868 (Beolens & Watkins, 2003, pp. 29) (myrmecocichla, arnot's chat, 302, 957) H. B. Tristram, 1869.

arquata L. bow-shaped, curved, arched; *arcus* bow, arc, arch, rainbow; in the case of the thrush it refers to the black mark on chest and in the case of the curlew reference is to the curved beak (cichladusa, collared palm-thrush, 312, 935, W. Peters, 1835) (numenius, eurasian curlew, 170, 350, C. Linnaeus, 1758).

arquatrix L. jaundiced, jaundice sufferer for the yellow orbital skin of the bird; *arcus* rainbow (columba, african olive-pigeon, 200, 278) C. J. Temminck, 1808.

arundinaceus L. resembling a reed; *arundo* or *harundo* reed, arrow, pen, shepherd's pipe; the suffix -*aceus* means resembling (acrocephalus, great reed-warbler, 320, 799) C. Linnaeus, 1758.

asiaticus from Asia, the largest and most populous continent on earth; probably from Assyrian word *asu* East or Sanskrit *usa* dawn; oldest use of the word is Gr. Asia (Ἀσία) and it denoted all the countries that lied in the East; in Greek mythology it was the name of a Nymph or Titan, goddess of Lydia; the common name of the bird refers to the Caspian Sea, the largest body of water by area in the world, where the bird breeds; the name of the lake derives from a tribe that used to live in the area (charadrius, caspian plover, 152, 406) P. S. Pallas, 1773.

asio both Jobling and Roberts agree it means owl; Jobling claims it is L. and Roberts it is Gr.; in Gr. *asios* (ἄσιος) means full of mud from *asis* (ἄσις) mud (33)

assimilis L. similar, close resembling; indicates a close resemblance or relationship to another species (puffinus, little shearwater, 42, 676) J. Gould, 1838.

astrild L. Roberts claims it means a star or starred, probably from L. *astrum* and Gr. *astron* (ἄστρον); Jobling (2010, pp. 57) though reports that *astrild derives from a German or Dutch avicultural term for a waxbill* but he also mentions Reichenbach's comments: '*Astrild seems to have been a misprint for astrilda, which might be restored as having a more classical appearance*' (estrilda, common waxbill, 396, 1051) C. Linnaeus, 1758.

atlantisia from Atlantis; the island state mentioned in two works by Plato; Atlantis was never mentioned before Plato but it has become very popular and many writers refer to it as if it were real; it is placed somewhere in the Atlantic ocean; both Atlantis and the ocean are named after Atlas, the Titan, punished by Zeus to carry the heavens on his shoulders (not the earth) after the Titans were defeated by the Gods (Sinclair et al. 414).

atricapilla L. black haired or black-capped; *ater* black; *capillus* hair (of head or beard) (sylvia, blackap, 314, 818) C. Linnaeus, 1758.

atricollis L. black-necked; *ater* black; *collum, -i* neck (ortygospiza, african qualfinch, 398, 1040) L. J. P. Vieillot, 1817.

atrocaerulea L. dark blue; *ater* black; *caeruleus* blue (hirundo, blue swallow, 280, 752) C. J. Sundevall, 1850.

atrococcineus L and Gr. black and red; *ater* black; *coccino* (κόκκινο) red; *coccum* scarlet

dye, dress; the word for red in Gr. comes from the pip of holly or yew; it came to mean red because the pips were used to dye red (laniarius, crimson-breasted shrike, 358, 699) W. J. Burchell, 1822.

atrogularis L. black throated; *ater* black, dark; *gula, -ae* throat (crithagra, black-throated canary, 406, 1120) A. Smith, 1836.

audeberti after *Audebert*, who first recorded and collected the specimen in Madagascar; three different first names are found for Audebert, namely, M or J. B or Fr Alphonso! Jean Baptiste was a miniature painter and worked with L. J. P. Vieillot but doesn't seem to be connected to the cuckoo in any way (pachycoccyx, thick-billed cuckoo, 214, 204) H. Schlegel, 1879.

augur L. prophet or soothsayer; after the augur, a priest in ancient Rome, who interpreted the will of Gods by studying the flight of birds and especially of eagles, hawks and owls (buteo, augur buzzard, 104, 525) E. Rüppell, 1836.

aurantius L. orange-coloured, in reference to underpart

coloration; the common name of the bird refers to the 1000 km long mountain range that takes its name from Afrikaans and it means 'dragon mountains' (chaetops, dragensberg rock-jumper, 300, 735) E.L. Layard, 1867.

auratus L. golden, ornamented with gold; *aurum* gold (oriolus, african golden oriole, 286, 680) L. J. P. Vieillot, 1817.

auritus L. eared, long eared; *auris* ear, hearing, listener (nettapus, african pygmy-goose, 80, 99) P. Boddaert, 1783.

australis L. southern; *auster* south, south wind; Gr. *ao, aemi* (ἄω, ἄημι) to blow (eremopterix, black-eared sparrowlark, 272, 885, A. Smith, 1836) (hyliota, southern hyliota, 344, 809, G. E. Shelley, 1882) (lamprotornis, burchell's starling, 368, 966, A. Smith, 1836) (tchagra, brown-crowned tchagra, 360, 693, A. Smith, 1836).

aviceda L. bird killing or killing bird; *avis* bird, omen; *caedere* to kill; *caedes,-is slaughter, murder;* Fr. *avion* Eng. *avi*ation (39)

avosetta Venetian or Italian name for the pied avocet (recurvirostra, pied avocet, 150, 392) C. Linnaeus, 1758.

axillaris L. of the shoulder or armpit; *axilla* armpit; Eng. axil (euplectes, fan-tailed widowbird, 390, 1031) A. Smith, 1838.

ayresii/ayresi after Thomas *Ayres* (1828-1913), a British-born collector, naturalist, hunter, beer-brewer and gold prospector who lived in Australia for a short while but settled in South Africa (aquila, Ayres's hawk-eagle, 98, 534, J. H. Gurney Sr, 1862) (cisticola, wing-snapping cisticola, 330, 842, G. Hartlaub, 1863) (sarothrura, red-chested flufftail, 140, 321, J. H. Gurney Sr, 1877).

B

baboecala Gr. chatterer; *vavax, vavakos (βάβαξ, βάβακος)* chatterer, loudmouth; *vavazo (βαβάζω)* is the verb *to chat*; Vavax was a knickname of Pan, the god of the wild in Greek mythology (bradypterus, little rush-warbler, 316, 792) L. J. P. Vieillot, 1817.

badius L. chestnut coloured, reddish-brown; of the six

subspecies, A.b. polyzonoides is the one found in the region; Gr. *polyzonoides* means many girdles or many bands; Shikra means hunter in Hindi (accipiter, shikra, 110, 514). J.F. Gmelin, 1788.

baeticatus L. clothed in wool from *Baetica*, a roman province (now Andalusia), from the ancient name of the river Guadalquivir, Baetis (acrocephalus, african reed-warbler, 318, 797). L. J. P. Vieillot, 1817.

bailloni after Jean Francois Emmanuel *Baillon* (1744-1802), a lawyer, collector and naturalist from Abbeville, France (puffinus, tropical shearwater, 42, 676) C. L. Bonaparte, 1857.

bairdii after Spencer Fullerton *Baird* (1823-1887), an American zoologist and ornithologist; he organised expeditions with the *Albatross* and was assistant Secretary and then Secretary of the Smithsonian Institution, whose collection of natural history collections he increased from 6,000 specimens to over 2 million between 1850 and the time of his death; he wrote a *Catalogue of North American Birds* in 1858 and more than 1,000 works during his lifetime;

he was also Coues' mentor (calidris, baird's sandpiper, 164, 370) E. Coues, 1861.

balaenarum L. pertaining to a whale, of the whales; *balaena, -ae* whale; *balaena* whale; refers to Walvis Bay, Namibia; Afrikaans *Walvisbaai* and Dutch *Walvisch Baai* Whale Bay (sterna, damara tern, 194, 464) H. E. Strickland, 1852.

balearica after the *Balearic Islands*, Spain; Pliny mentions a bird without any other details; maybe in ancient times one of the cranes migrated as north as Tunisia or the Nile valley; the name Balearic comes from Gr. or Phoenician; in Gr. it would derive from the people's skills as slingers (*baleareis* βαλλεαρείς from verb *vallo* βάλλω to launch); the Phoenician version would mean the islanders believed in Baal and the resemblance to the Gr. word is accidental (34).

baraui after Armand *Barau* (1921-1989), co-author in 1982 with Nicolas Barré and Christian H. Jouanin of *Oiseaux de la Réunion*, the first study of the birds of that island; he was a landowner and amateur ornithologist on the island (pterodroma, barau's petrel, 36, 660) C. Jouanin, 1964.

barbatus L. bearded; *barba* beard, chin; Eng. *barb*er (apus, african black swift, 228, 238, P. L. Sclater, 1865) (gypaetus, bearded vulture, 88, 484, C. Linnaeus, 1758).

barlowi after Charles Sydney 'Punch' *Barlow* (1905-1979) a South African entrepreneur, philanthropist, sportsman and lover of nature; he was a friend of Dr Austin Roberts and chairman of the John Voelcker Bird Book Fund until his death in 1979; it originally raised the funds for the publication of The Birds of Southern Africa; he sponsored the 1937 Barlow-Rand ornithological expedition to the west of southern Afrca (calendulauda, barlow's lark, 268, 874) Roberts, 1937.

barrati after F. A. Barratt (ca 1847-1875), collector in the Transvaal, South Africa; he collected the specimen and sent it to the British Museum (bradypterus, 316, 794) R. B. Sharpe, 1876.

barrowi after Sir John *Barrow* 1st Baronet (1764-1848), an English statesman and writer;

after working in China he moved to South Africa and then back to England to become Second Secretary to the Admiralty, a post he held for the next forty years and became a great promoter of Arctic voyages of discovery; several geographical features are named after him, such as Barrow Point, Alaska and Barrow Strait, Canada; he never visited any of the places named after him (eupodotis, barrow's korhaan, 148, 304 E. senegalensis barrowii) J. E. Gray, 1829.

batis Gr. a worm-eating bird mentioned by Aristotle with no further identification; in Gr. *batis* (μπάτης) means breeze and derives from the word *emvaino* (ἐμβαίνω) to enter (49).

belcheri after Sir Charles Frederic *Belcher* (1876-1970), an Australian lawyer, author, and amateur ornithologist; he served the British Colonial Service in Africa, Cyprus and West Indies; he was a founding member of the Royal Australasian Ornithologists Union and the Bird Observers Club (pachyptila, slender-billed prion, 34, 665) G. Mathews, 1912.

bellicosus L. warlike, fierce, fond of war, aggressive, martial; *bellum* war, warfare, battle, combat, fight; an expression still used in many languages is *casus belli* reason for war (polemaetus, martial eagle, 96, 538) F. M. Daudin, 1800.

bengalensis/benghalensis from Bengal; Bengal is a region that part belongs to India and part to Bangladesh, since 1947; it is one of the most densely populated areas in the world; the name বাংলা *Bangla* (Bengali) and বঙ্গ *Bongo* (Bengal) derives either from the Dravidian-speaking tribe of Bang or from the kingdom of Vanga during the time of Mahabharata in the region of Bengal (rostratula, greater painted-snipe, 172, 380, C. Linnaeus, 1758) (sterna, lesser crested tern, 190, 452 R. Lesson, 1831).

benguelensis from Benguela; Benguela is the name of a city and a province in Angola and also the name of an ocean current that extends from Cape Point all the way to Angola and its full of nutrients cold waters sustain huge amounts of phytoplankton and the Benguela ecosystem (certhilauda, benguela long-billed lark, 262, 883) R. B. Sharpe, 1904.

bennettii after Edward Turner *Bennett* (1797-1836), an English surgeon, zoologist and writer; Bennett promoted the setting up of a London entomological club which developed in the zoological society in connection with the Linnean Society; he became its first vice-secretary and later secretary until his premature death at the age of 39; he wrote *The Tower Menagerie, The Gardens and Menagerie of the Zoological Society* among other works; he co-authored with G.T. Lay the Fishes' section in the *Zoology of Beechey's Voyage* (campethera, bennett's woodpecker, 258, 130) A. Smith, 1830.

bergii after Karl Heinrich *Bergius* (1790-1818), a Prussian botanist, naturalist, cavalryman and pharmacist who collected for the Berlin museum in southern Africa; he died in Cape Town of pulmonary tuberculosis (sterna, swift tern, 190, 453) M. Lichtenstein, 1823.

biarmicus L. two weapons; *bi* two, twice, double, having two; *armum, -i* arms, weapon, armor, shield, force; the origin of the name is obscure but some confusion with the old Norse name of an area in Russia *Bjarmaland* and latinised *Biarmia* has contributed to the name of this bird (falco, lanner falcon, 116, 556) C. J.Temminck, 1825.

bias Gr. a night bird, a species of owl; *buas (βύας)* a night bird, a species of owl, horn owl; Jobling (2010 pp. 71) claims it is Gr. bird of evil omen; Roberts (2009) says it is L. and means oblique, because of sloping crest (48).

bicinctus L. double girdled or banded; refers to the double breast bands; *bi* two, twice, double, having two; *cinctus* surrounded, encircled, enclosed, bordered; *cingere* surround, encircle, enclose, gird (pterocles, double-banded sandgrouse, 198, 340) C. J.Temminck, 1815.

bicolor L. of two colours, bicoloured, pied; *bi* two, twice, double, having two; *color* colour, pigment, shade, complexion (dendrocygna, white-faced duck, 80, 84, C. Linnaeus, 1766) (laniarius, swamp boubou, 360, 697, G. Hartlaub, 1857) (ploceus, dark-backed weaver, 382, 1020, L. J. P. Vieillot, 1819) (spermestes, red-backed mannikin, 404, 1068,

L. Fraser, 1843) (spreo, pied starling, 368, 968, J. F. Gmelin, 1789) (turdoides, southern pied babbler, 292, 811, W. Jardine, 1831).

bifasciata/bifasciatus L. double banded; *bi* two, twice, double, having two; *fascia* band, bandage, streak of clouds (cinnyris, purple-banded sunbird, 376, 1000, G. Shaw, 1811) (oenanthe, buff-streaked chat, 306, 947, C. J. Temminck, 1829).

bilineatus L. double-striped; *bi* two, twice, double, having two; *lineatus* striped, lined; *linea* line, string, boundary (pogoniulus, yellow-rumped tinkerbird, 254, 141) C. J. Sundevall, 1850.

blanchoti after François *Blanchot* de Verly (d. 1807), French Governor of Senegal (1787-1807) (Jobling, 2010, pp. 73) (malaconotus, grey-headed, 362, 706) J. F. Stephens, 1826.

boehmi after Richard *Böhm* (1854-1884), a German traveller and zoologist; he travelled to Zanzibar and East Africa, Tanzania and Zaire; he wrote articles for the Journal of Ornithology and *Ostafrika, Sansibar und Tanganjika heraus:*

Von Sansibar zum Tanganjika, Briefe aus Ostafrika von Dr. Richard Böhm, which was published in 1888; he discovered Lake Upemba and died at the age of 30 from malaria (merops, Böhm's bee-eater, 240, 190, A. Reichenow, 1882) (neafrapus, Böhm's spinetail, 230, 232, H. Schalow, 1882) (sarothrura, streaky-breasted flufftail, 140, 318, A. Reichenow, 1900).

borbonica after *Ile Bourbon,* the old name of Rèunion, the French island located in the Indian Ocean, east of Madagascar; it was named after the *House of Bourbon* in 1649 until 1793, when the name changed to Rèunion and then to Ile Bonaparte in 1801 and then to *Ile Bourbon* again in 1810 until 1848 and the fall of the restored Bourbons when the name once again changed to Rèunion (phedina, mascarene martin, 282, 746) J. F. Gmelin, 1789.

borin Italian name for the bird or another warbler from L. *bos, bovis* ox, bull, cow, cattle; it was reputed that the bird with this name kept close to cattle (Jobling, 2010, pp.75) (sylvia, garden warbler, 314, 819) P. Boddaert, 1783.

bostrychia Gr. curved, curly; *vostrychos (βόστρυχος)* lock of hair, small curl; *vostrychion (βοστρύχιον)* vine tentacle, octopus tentacle (43).

botaurus Gr. bellowing bull; *vous, voos (βοῦς, βοός)* ox in L. *bos, bovis* Eng. <u>bov</u>ine, *buffalo; taurus (ταῦρος)* bull; probably related to *tarvos (τάρβος)* fear (43).

brachypterus Gr. short-winged; *vrachys (βραχύς)* short; *pteron (πτερόν)* wing (cisticola, short-winged cisticola, 336, 837) R. B. Sharpe, 1870.

brachyura/us Gr. short-tailed; *vrachys (βραχύς)* short; *oura (οὐρά)* tail (anthus, short-tailed pipit, 354, 1111, C. J. Sundevall, 1850) (camaroptera, green-backed camaroptera, 322, 856, L. J. P. Vieillot, 1820).

bradfieldi after Rupert D, <u>Bradfield</u> (1882-1949), a South African farmer, naturalist and collector, who lived in Namibia for most of his life; he sent the hornbill to Austin Roberts and he named the bird after Bradfield; Bradfield had the southwest African endemic swift named after his wife (Beolens & Watkins, 2003, pp.

63) (apus, bradfield's swift, 228, 239, A. Roberts, 1926) (tockus, bradfield's hornbill, 246, 154, A. Roberts, 1930).

bradornis Gr. slow or sluggish bird; *vradys (βραδύς)* slow; *ornis ornithos (όρνις όρνιθος)* bird in ancient Gr.; the word for bird was both male and female in ancient Gr.; in modern Gr. it is female and it means chicken (54).

bradypterus Gr. slow-winged; *vradys (βραδύς)* slow, sluggish; *pteron (πτερόν)* wing (51).

brevicaudata L. short-tailed; *brevis* short, little, small, brief; *cauda* tail, penis; it actually means exactly the same as the other camaroptera in the region, only this bird takes its name from L. while the other one from Gr. (camaroptera, grey-backed camaroptera, 322, 856) P. J. Cretzschmar, 1830.

brevipes L. short-footed; *brevis* short, little, small, brief; *pes, pedis* foot (monticola, short-toed rock-thrush, 300, 899) G. R. Waterhouse, 1838.

brevirostris L. short-billed; *brevis* short, little, small, brief; *rostrum, rostri* bill, beak (certhilauda, agulhas long-billed lark, 262,

880, A. Roberts, 1941) (lugensa, kerguelen petrel, 38, 662, R. P. Lesson, 1831) (schoenicola, broad-tailed warbler, 316, 790, C. J. Sundevall, 1850).

brevis L. short, referring to the casque says Roberts (2009); *brevis* short, little, small, brief; (bycanistes, silvery-cheeked hornbill, 244, 157) H. Friedmann, 1829.

bubalornis Gr. buffalo bird; *boubalos (βούβαλος)* buffalo, cattle, ox; *ornis ornithos (όρνις όρνιθος)* bird in ancient Gr. Eng. ornitho-logy; it was observed that Red billed Buffalo weavers (*bubalornis niger*) followed herds of African buffalo (56).

bubo L. owl; *bubo, bubonis* horned or eagle owl (as bird of ill omen)(33).

bubulcus L. cowherd; *bubulcus* one who drives/tends cattle, plowman, rustic, farm labourer; *bubulus* of cattle, connected with cattle, of ox-hide (42).

bucinator L. trumpeter; *bucina, -ae* trumpet, sheperd's horn, nightwatch; Gr *voukane (βουκάνη)* (bycanistes, trumpeter hornbill, 244, 156) C. J. Temminck, 1824.

bucorvus Gr. & L. ox raven. Gr. *bous (βοῦς)* buffalo, cattle, ox; L. *corvus* raven, crow; *vuceros* (βούκερος) ox-horned, hornbill in Gr. (29).

bugeranus Gr. ox-crane or huge crane; *vous, voos (βοῦς, βοός)* buffalo, cattle, ox; *geranos (γερανός)* crane (34).

bulleri after Sir Walter Lawry <u>Buller</u> (1838-1906), a New Zealand barrister, naturalist and dominant ornithologist; his *History of the birds of New Zealand* became a New Zealand classic; he tried to sell a laughing owl to Rothchild but he was exposed as the bird was fake (thalassarche, buller's albatross, 28, 648) L. W. Rothschild, 1893.

bullockoides resembling *merops bullocki, red-throated bee-eater*; after William <u>Bullock</u> (1773-1849), an English naturalist, entrepreneur and collector who published several pamphlets on natural history; Gr. *-oides (-οειδές)* resembling (merops, white-fronted bee-eater, 238, 186) A. Smith, 1834.

bulweria /bulwerii after Reve James <u>Bulwer</u> (1794-1879), an English collector, naturalist and conchologist (he who studies mollusc shells from Gr. *konkhos* κόγχος 'cockle'); Bulwer collected the petrel in Madeira and it was named after him as was the genus *bulweria* (bulweria, bulwer's petrel, 44, 667) W. Jardine & P. J. Selby, 1828.

buphagus Gr. cattle or ox-eater; *vous, voos (βοῦς, βοός)* buffalo, cattle, ox; *phagein (φαγεῖν)* to eat (infinitive of *ephagon* έφαγον (I ate) with no present but *esthio* (ἐσθίω) I eat); in Gr. mythology, Buphagus, was an Arcadian hero who helped Iphicles, Hercules's brother; he was later killed by Artemis, goddess of hunting; it was also the nickname of Hercules and others, who had supposedly eaten a whole bull at once (55).

burchelli/burchellii after William John <u>Burchell</u> (1781-1863), an English explorer, naturalist, artist and author; he travelled in South Africa and Brasil, where he collected thousands of specimens; his writings from Brasil are lost and his Southafrican expeditions are described in his *Travels in the Interior of Southern Africa;* among other species, he was the first to describe the white rhinoceros (*Ceratotherium simum*) and his name was given to the common or Burchell's zebra (*equus burchelli);* he became very ill the last two years of his life and eventually took his own life (centropus, burchell's coucal, 218, 220, W. J. Swainson, 1838) (pterocles, burchell's sandgrouse, 198, 341, W. L. Sclater, 1922).

burhinus Gr. buffalo nose meaning large or great nose; *vous, voos (βοῦς, βοός)* buffalo, cattle, ox; *rhis, rhinos (ρίς, ρινός)* nose (for men and animals alike) (37).

burra *burrus* old form of *Pyrrhus* (Gr. *pyrrhos* πυρρός red), usually for people with red hair like the Scythians (calendulauda, red lark, 268, 871) O. Bangs, 1930.

buteo L. species of hawk; *buteo, buteonis* falco, buzzard; Gr. *triorkhes* a hawk mentioned by Aristophanes, probably *falco buteo* and it means *he who has three testicles*!(40).

butorides L. bittern-like; *butorides* bittern-like; *botor* heron-like bird from *butor* and *butitaurus* bittern + taurus (bull) due to its booming voice (42).

bycanistes Gr. trumpeter; *vycanistes* (βυκανιστής)

trumpeter; *vycane (βυκάνη)* trumpet *vycanao (βυκανάω)* to blow the trumpet (29).

C

cabanisi after Jean Louis Cabanis (1816-1906), a German ornithologist; he was assistant and later director of the Berlin University Museum and founded the *Journal für Ornithologie* in 1853 and edited it until 1894; he never visited Africa but only North America; Anton Reichenow, who was his son in law, succeded him as editor of the *Journal* and he named the bunting after Cabanis (emberiza, cabani's bunting, 412, 1138) A. Reichenow, 1875.

caerulea/caeruleus L. blue or sky blue; *caeruleus* blue, dark blue, sky blue, cerulean, azure (egretta, little blue heron, 64, 584, C. Linnaeus, 1758) (elanus, black-shouldered kite, 112, 478, R. L. Desfontaines, 1789) (halobaena, blue petrel, 32, 662, J. F. Gmelin, 1789).

caerulescens L. bluish; *caeruleus* blue, dark blue, sky blue, cerulean, azure (eupodotis, blue korhaan, 148, 302, L. J. P. Vieillot, 1820) (muscicapa, ashy flycatcher, 340, 921, G. Hartlaub, 1865) (rallus, african rail, 138, 323, J. F. Gmelin, 1789).

caesia L. bluish grey, blue-eyed; *caesius* grey, grey-blue, steel-coloured, steel-coloured, having grey/gey-blue/steel-coloured eyes (coracina, grey cuckooshrike, 284, 732) M. Lichtenstein, 1823.

caffra/caffer Southafrican, from Kaffraria; Kaffraria was the name of the southeastern part of South Africa; from the Arabic word *kaffir* infidel; first used by Arabs to describe black people who didn't believe in Allah and then the Portuguese used it to describe the black non muslims of eastern Africa; it had no derogatory meaning; it was used in a derogatory meaning by whites in South Africa, especially during the Apartheid era; a statement during a sitting of the South African Parliament in 2008 describes how the word is viewed in the country today: *'We should take care not to use derogatory words that were used to demean black persons in this country. Words such as Kaffir, coolie, Boesman, hotnot and many others have negative connotations and remain offensive as they were used to degrade, undermine and strip South Africans of their humanity and dignity'* (anthus, bushveld pipit, 354, 1112, C. J. Sundevall, 1850) (apus, white-rumped swift, 230, 243, M. Lichtenstein, 1823) (cossypha, cape robin-chat, 310, 928, C. Linnaeus, 1771) (promerops, cape sugarbird, 372, 1002, C. Linnaeus, 1758).

cailliauti after Frédéric *Cailliaud* (1787-1869), a French naturalist, mineralogist and curator of the Natural History Museum of his birthplace, Nantes, France; he travelled in Egypt and Sudan, looking for gold for Muhammad Ali (1769-1849), the Albanian ruler of Egypt; he wrote beautiful descriptions of the area and the people he found there; he published a lot about the nature of the area and his encyclopaedia of the peoples of the area was lost and found only a few years ago (campethera, green-backed woodpecker, 256, 133) A. Malherbe, 1849.

calamonastes Gr. reed singer; *kalamos (κάλαμος) (kalami (καλάμι)* in modern Gr.) reed; *astes* singer; *ado (ἄδω)* sing (52).

callandrella Gr. small lark; diminutive of *kalandros (κάλανδρος)* lark (53).

calendulauda combination of two lark genera, *calendula* and *alauda*; *calendula* diminutive of *kalandros (κάλανδρος)* lark; *calendula is a substantive which may be formed from the gerund of the verb 'caleo' I am warm; figuratively, glowing; in allusion to the fiery colour on the head; it was apparently coined by Brisson, 1760, for the European Regulus cristatus but was in 1766 appropriated by Linnaeus to the present species* (Jobling, 2010, pp. 84) *alauda* lark; *according to Pliny this was the Celtic name, meaning 'great songstress,' for the lark (al = great, aud= song)* (Jobling, 2010, pp. 37) (53).

calidris Gr. *kalidris (καλίδρις)* or skalidris *(σκαλίδρις)*, a waterside bird with spots mentioned by Aristotle, probably *scolopax calidris* (36).

calonectris Gr. good swimmer; *kalos (καλός)* good; *nectris (νηκτρίς)* female of *nektes (νήκτης)* swimmer; *nekho (νήχω)* swim (46).

calvus L. bald (geronticus, southern bald ibis, 76, 610, P. Boddaert, 1783) (treron, african green-pigeon, 204, 290, C. J. Temminck, 1810).

camaroptera Gr. arched wings; *kamara (καμάρα)* arch; *pteron (πτερόν)* (*ftero φτερό* in modern Gr) wing (52).

camelus L. camel; from Hebrew *gamal* where Gr. *kamelos (κάμηλος)* and L. *camelus* derive (struthio, common osrich, 124, 60) C. Linnaeus, 1758.

campephaga Gr. caterpillar-eating; *kampe (κάμπη)* and in modern Gr. *kampia (κάμπια)* caterpillar; *phagein (φαγεῖν)* to eat (infinitive of *ephagon ἔφαγον* (I ate) with no present but *esthio ἐσθίω* I eat) (48).

campethera Gr. caterpillar-hunting; *kampe (κάμπη)* and in modern Gr. *kampia (κάμπια)* caterpillar; thera *(θήρα)* hunting wild animals; *therao (θηράω)* to hunt wild animals (28).

cana L. grey, hoary, old; *referring to head of drake* (Roberts, 2009); *canus, cana* grey, hoary, old, grey-haired, wise (tadorna, south african shelduck, 78, 93) J. F. Gmelin, 1789.

canicollis L. grey-necked; *canus, cana* grey, hoary, old, grey-haired; *collum* neck (serinus, cape canary, 408, 1116) W. J. Swainson, 1838.

canorus L. melodious; *canorus* melodious, musical; *canere* to sing, to recite, to play an instrument, foretell; *canor, canoris* sound, melody (cuculus, common cuckoo, 212, 207, C. Linnaeus, 1758) (melierax, southern pale chanting hawk, 112, 509, Rislachi, 1799 (Roberts, 2009) or C. P. Thunberg, 1799).

cantans L. singing; *cantare* to sing, praise, pretend; *cantator, -oris singer* (cisticola, singing cisticola, 334, 825) T. von Heuglin, 1896.

canutus after, <u>Canute</u>, king of England, Denmark & Norway (985 or 995-1035); Jobling (2010, pp. 89) reports that King Canute *regarded the Red Knot, suitably fattened with white bread and milk, as a delicacy*; King Cnut the Great was the son of Danish Prince Sweyn Forkbeard; he ruled England for nineteen years; he brought together the English and Danish kingdoms and also reigned across Scandinavia, considered by many a wise King and statesman; there are six subspecies recognised and the one to be found in southern Africa is calidris c. canutus (calidris, red knot, 162, 362) C. Linnaeus, 1758.

capense/capensis after the <u>Cape</u> of Good Hope, South Africa; originally named *'Cape of Storms'* (Cabo das tormentas) by Bartholomeu Diaz, renamed *'Cabo da Boa Esperança'* (Cape of Good Hope) by King John II of Portugal (anas, cape teal, 84, 101, J. F. Gmelin, 1789) (asio, marsh owl, 220, 263, A. Smith, 1834)(batis, cape batis, 346, 713, C. Linnaeus, 1766)(bubo, cape eagle-owl, 222, 255, A. Smith, 1834)(burhinus, spotted thick-knee, 178, 387, M. Lichtenstein, 1823) (corvus, cape crow, 288, 722, M. Lichtenstein, 1823) (daption, pintado petrel, 32, 658, C. Linnaeus, 1758) (emberiza, cape bunting, 412, 1135, C. Linnaeus, 1766) (euplectes, yellow bishop, 390, 1030, C. Linnaeus, 1766) (glaucidium, african barred owlet, 220, 262, A. Smith, 1834) (macronyx, cape longclaw, 356, 1098, C. Linnaeus, 1766) (microparra, lesser jacana, 136, 383, A. Smith, 1839) (morus, cape gannet, 52, 565, M. Lichtenstein, 1823) (motacilla, cape wagtail, 348, 1091, C. Linnaeus, 1766) (oena, namaqua dove, 204, 289, C. Linnaeus, 1766) (phalacrocorax, cape cormorant, 54, 579, A. E. Sparrman, 1788) (ploceus, cape weaver, 386, 1012, C. Linnaeus, 1766) (pternistis, cape spurfowl, 126, 71, J. F.

Gmelin, 1789) (pycnonotus, cape bulbul, 294, 769, C. Linnaeus, 1766) (smithornis, african broadbill, 232, 678, A. Smith, 1839) (tyto, african grass-owl, 222, 252, A. Smith, 1834)

capicola L. inhabitant of the Cape; *colere* to dwell, to inhabit (streptopelia, cape turtle-dove, 202, 284) C. J. Sundevall, 1857.

caprimulgus L. goat milker; *capra* goat; *mulgere* to milk; Gr. *amelgo (αμέλγω)* to milk; Pliny reports that goat-suckers caused goats to go blind! (33).

caprius L. goat-like; the name means nothing but was erroneously attributed to this bird; the original name was *cupreus* coppery, but later that name was given to the African Emerald Cuckoo and so it stayed; its common name looks like a name but it's not; it's onomatopoeic (chrysococcyx, diderick cuckoo, 216, 214) P. Boddaert, 1783.

cardinalis L. cardinal; senior church leader of the Roman Catholic church who wears a scarlet cap; cardinals are ordained bishops and among other duties they also elect the Pope (quelea, cardinal quelea, 388, 1023) G. Hartlaub, 1880.

carneipes L. flesh-footed, or flesh-coloured foot; *caro, carnis* meat, corpse, flesh (Italian *carne*); *pes, pedis* foot (puffinus, flesh-footed shearwater, 40, 672) J. Gould, 1844.

caroli after *Carolus* (Karl or Charles) Johan (John) Andersson (1827-1867), a Swedish explorer, hunter, trader, naturalist, collector and ornithologist; he published many books about his travels and explorations mainly in modern-day Namibia; in 1850 he went to Africa for the first time, returned to London in 1855 but went back to Africa the same year; he wrote *Lake Ngami, The Okavango River, The Lion and The Elephant*; he died in Angola at the age of 40 (anthoscopus, grey penduline-tit, 324, 737) R.B. Sharpe, 1871.

carpi after Bernhard *Carp* (1901-1966), a Dutch-born South African businessman, naturalist and sponsor of collecting expeditions of the Zoological Museum of Amsterdam University, mainly to Namibia; his autobiography was entitled *Why I chose Africa*; the tit was collected in 1951 and was originally considered a subspecies of *Parus niger* (Beolens & Watkins, 2003, pp.

77) (parus, carp's tit, 292, 739) Macdonald & Hall, 1957.

carteri after Thomas *Carter* (1863-1931) an English ornithologist who collected and wrote extensively on birds in Western Australia; four species and fourteen subspecies are named after him; he collected and identified a number of birds in the area (Beolens & Watkins, 2003, pp. 77) (thalassarche, indian yellow-nosed albatross, 28, 652) L. W. Rothschild, 1903.

carunculatus L. wattled; *caruncula* piece of flesh; diminutive of *caro, carnis* meat, corpse, flesh and also colourless speech; Eng. *carn*ival, *carn*ivore (bugeranus, wattled crane, 142, 311) J. F. Gmelin, 1789.

caspia of the Caspian sea; the Caspian Sea, (Ru. Каспийское море) is the largest lake in the world; it lies to the east of Mount Caucasus and to the west of the steppe of Central Asia; it has no outflows; the name derives from the tribe of Caspi, already gone at the time of Strabo; Greeks and Persians called it the Hyrcanian Ocean and Turcic people call it the sea of the Khazars, an empire based to the south of the lake in the late first millennium of our

era (sterna, caspian tern, 188, 450) P. S. Pallas, 1770.

catharacta Gr. cascade; *katarakhtes (καταρράχτης)* cascade, torrent; a waterbird, thus named for its manner of attacking (Aristophanes); *katareo (καταρρέω)* to flow downwards; Eng. *cataract* (38).

cauta L. shy, cautious; *cautus* cautious, careful, prudent, on guard, safe; passive perfect participle of *cavere* to beware, to guard against, beware, avoid; Eng. cover, covert (thalassarche, shy albatross, 24, 646) J. Gould, 1841.

centropus Gr. spike foot; *kentron* or *kentri (κέντρον ή κεντρί)* spike; pous, podos *(ποῦς, ποδός)* foot (31).

cercococcyx Gr. cuckoo tail; *kerkos (κέρκος)* animal tail; *coccyx (κόκκυξ)* cuckoo from its cry *kokky (κόκκυ)* in Gr. used as an exclamation meaning Forward! Quickly! (31).

cercomela Gr. black-tailed; *kerkos (κέρκος)* animal tail; *melas μέλας* black, dark, dusky (55).

cercotrichas Gr. tailed-thrush; *kerkos (κέρκος)* animal tail; *trihas τριχάς* thrush (54).

certhilauda combination of genus *Certhia* and *Alauda; kerthios (κέρθιος)* small insectivorous bird mentioned by Aristotle *certhia familiaris; alauda* lark; *according to Pliny this was the Celtic name, meaning 'great songstress,' for the lark (al = great, aud= song)* (Jobling, 2010, pp. 37) (53).

cervinus L. deer, deer-coloured, reddish brown, pertaining to a stag; *cervus, -i* deer, male deer, forked branches (anthus, red-throated pipit, 354, 1114) P. S. Pallas, 1811.

ceryle Gr. kingfisher; *kerylos (κειρύλος)* or *(κηρύλος)* kingfisher (30).

ceuthmochares Gr. happy to hide; *kephthmos* or *kefthmon, kefthmonos (κευθμός ή κευθμών, κευθμόνος)* hole, den, hiding; *khairo (χαίρω)* to be happy, to enjoy, to take pleasure; the word in correct ancient Gr. would be *ceuthmonochares (κευθμονοχαρής)* (31).

chaetops Gr. bristle eye or hair on face; *khaite (χαίτη)* hair; *opsis (ὄψις)* face or *ops, opos (ὤψ, ὠπός)* eye, face (49).

chalcomitra Gr. wearing a bronze or copper head-band or cap; *khalcos χαλκός* copper; *mitra* head-band, cap (56).

chalcopterus Gr. copper or bronze-winged; *khalcos χαλκός* copper; *pteron πτερόν (ftero φτερό* in modern Gr) wing (rhinoptilus, bronze-winged courser, 180, 422) C. J. Temminck, 1824.

chalcospilos Gr. copper-spotted; *khalcos (χαλκός)* copper; *spilos (σπίλος)* spot, stain, blemish (turtur, emerald-spotted wood-dove, 132, 287) J. G. Wagler, 1827.

chalybaeus/chalybeus/ chalybeata Gr. steely; *khalyps, -vos (χάλυψ, -βος)* tempered iron, steel; Chalybes (Χάλυβες) was a people in Asia Minor famed for their ability to work iron and the Greek name passed into Latin as *chalybs* (cinnyris, southern double-coloured sunbird, 376, 988, C. Linnaeus, 1766) (lamprotornis, greater blue-eared starling, 366, 964, W. Hemprich & C. G. Ehrenberg, 1828) (vidua, village indigobird, 394, 1076, P. L. Statius Müller, 1776).

charadrius Gr. plover; *kharadrios (χαραδριός)* yellowish bird living in ravines according to

Sundevall; a stone-curlew or thick-kneed bustard *charadrius oedicnemus*; Ancient Greeks considered it very greedy hence the saying for a glutton *living the life of a kharadrios (χαραδριοῦ βίον ζῆν);* another story about this bird was that people with jaundice were cured if they saw it; *kharadra (χαράδρα)* ravine, gorge (37).

chelicuti of Chelicut; *Chelicut* a location in Ethiopia (Jobling mentions *it is east of Antalo and south of Makalo, Tigre, Abyssinia,* 2010, pp. 100) where Edward, Lord Stanley obtained the type specimen which he described in his *Salt's Voyage to Abyssinia* (halcyon, striped kingfisher, 236, 182) E. Smith-Stanley, 1814.

cheniana from *Chenyane* or *Tshwenyane* Hills, north of Zeerust in the Transvaal or Singuni name *Tsiyana* for a small brown bird, probably a sort of warbler (Jobling, 2010, pp. 100) (mirafra, melodious lark, 264, 861) A. Smith, 1843.

chersomanes Gr. fond of barren land; *khersos (χέρσος)* barren land; *manes (μανής)* passionately fond of; *mainomai (μαίνομαι)* to rage; Eng. *mania; khersomaneo (χερσομανέω)* to

become enraged like barren land (53).

chicquera presumably derives from Hindi *shikra* शिकारी hunter or it was erroneously identified as a shikra and the name *chicquera* stayed with it (falco, red-necked falcon, 116, 550) F. M. Daudin, 1800.

chiniana from *Chenyane* or *Tshwenyane* Hills, north of Zeerust in the Transvaal or Singuni name *Tsiyana* for a small brown bird, probably a sort of warbler (Jobling, 2010, pp. 101) (cisticola, rattling cisticola, 332, 827) A. Smith, 1843.

chionis Gr. snow, white ; *chion, chionos (χιών, χιόνος)* and in modern Gr. *chioni (χιόνι)* snow (37).

chirindensis of Chirinda forest; Chirinda forest lies on the slopes of Mount Selinda in Manicaland, Zimbabwe; it means lookout or vantage point or place of refuge in chiNdau; *rinda* means guard in Shona (apalis, chirinda apalis, 326, 855) G. E. Shelley, 1906.

chlidonias Gr. swallow-like; *khelidon (χελιδών)* swallow; *khlidon, khlidonos (χλίδων,* χλίδωνος) a jewel for the arms, neck or legs (39).

chloris Gr. yellow-green, green; *khloros (χλωρός)* yellow-green, green, fresh, not dry; *khloris (χλωρίς)* a pale-bellied bird, the size of *alauda (galerida) cristata* mentioned by Aristotle; *Chloris* in Greek mythology was a nymph associated with plants, trees, flowers, spring and new growth (anthus, yellow-breasted pipit, 356, 1100) M. Lichtenstein, 1842.

chlorocephalus Gr. green-headed; *khloros (χλωρός)* yellow-green, green, fresh, not dry; *cephale (κεφαλή* ancient Gr.; *κεφάλι* in modern Gr.) head (oriolus, green-headed oriole, 286, 681) G. E. Shelley, 1896.

chlorocichla Gr. green thrush; *khloros (χλωρός)* yellow-green, green, fresh, not dry; *kikhle* or *cichla (κίχλη* or *τσίχλα)* thrush. (50).

chloropeta Gr. green or yellow flyer; *khloros (χλωρός)* yellow-green, green, fresh, not dry; *petomai (πέτομαι)* to fly (51).

chloropus Gr. green-footed; *khloros (χλωρός)* yellow-green, green, fresh, not dry; *pous, podos*

(πούς, ποδός) foot or leg; *podi (πόδι)* in Modern Gr. (gallinula, common moorhen, 134, 334) C. Linnaeus, 1758.

chlororhynchos Gr. green or yellow-billed; *khloros (χλωρός)* yellow-green, green, fresh, not dry; *rynchos (ρύγχος) bill, beak, snout;* (thalassarche, atlantic yellow-nosed albatross, 28, 651) J. F. Gmelin, 1789.

chroicocephalus Gr. coloured head; *chrozo (χρώζω)* to colour, to stain; *cephale (κεφαλή* ancient Gr.; *κεφάλι* modern Gr.) head.

chrysococcyx Gr. golden cuckoo; *khrysos (χρυσός)* gold; *coccyx (κόκκυξ)* cuckoo from its cry *kokky (κόκκυ)* in Gr. used as an exclamation meaning Forward! Quickly! (31).

chrysocome Gr. golden-haired; *khrysos (χρυσός)* gold; *kome* κόμη hair; in Greek mythology it was a name attributed to Apollo, son of Zeus and Leto, god of light, music, medicine, prophecy and truth (*ό χρυσοκόμας* Φοîβος Aristophanes, Birds, 217) (eudyptes, rockhopper penguin, 16, 631) J. R. Forster, 1781.

chrysoconus Gr. golden cone; *khrysos (χρυσός)* gold; *konos* *(κῶνος)* cone; should have been *kome* (κόμη) or L. *komus* hair (Roberts, 2005, pp. 142) (pogoniulus, yellow-fronted tinkerbird, 254, 142) C. J. Temminck, 1832.

chrysolophus Gr. golden-crested; *khrysos (χρυσός)* gold; *lophion (λοφίον)* crest (eudyptes, macaroni penguin, 16, 630) J. F. von Brandt, 1837.

chrysostoma Gr. golden mouth; *khrysos (χρυσός)* gold; *stoma* (στόμα) mouth (thalassarche, grey-headed albatross, 26, 650) J. R. Forster, 1785.

chuana after Chuana (Tswana) *Chue* or *Chui* was a water-hole northeast of Latakoo(=Takoon) (Jobling, 2010, pp. 106) or from Tswana people (certhilauda, short-clawed lark, 260, 884) A. Smith, 1836.

chukar the name comes from the Sanskrit *chakor* or *chukor* (alectoris, chukar partridge, 128, 61) J. E. Gray, 1830.

cichladusa Gr. singing thrush; *kikhle* κίχλη thrush (*cichla* (τσίχλα) thrush in modern Gr.); *adousa (ἄδουσα)* singing; *ado* (ἄδω) to sing (54).

ciconia L. stork, swan (ciconia, white stork, 70, 623) C. Linnaeus, 1758.

cincta/cinctus L. banded or girdled; *cingere* to encircle; Gr. *kinglis (κιγκλίς)* iron gate (rhinoptilus, three-banded courser, 180, 423, T. von Heuglin, 1863) (riparia, banded martin, 282, 745, P. Boddaert, 1783).

cinerascens L. ashen; *cinis, cineris* ash, ruins; (circaetus, western banded snake-eagle, 92, 497, J. W. von Müller) (parus, ashy tit, 290, 742, L. J. P. Vieillot, 1818).

cinerea/cinereus L. ash-grey, ash-coloured; *cinis, cineris* ash, ruins; (ardea, grey heron, 62, 587, C. Linnaeus, 1758) (calandrella, red-capped lark, 260, 889, J. F. Gmelin, 1789) (circaetus, brown snake-eagle, 92, 494, L. J. P. Vieillot, 1818) (creatophora, wattled starling, 370, 970, F. C. Meuschen, 1787) (motacilla, grey wagtail, 348, 1095, Tunstall, 1771) (procellaria, grey petrel, 38, 669, J. F. Gmelin, 1789) (xenus, terek sandpiper, 166, 359, J. A. Güldenstädt, 1774-5).

cinnamomeiventris L. cinnamon-coloured belly; *cinnamomum* cinnamon Gr.

kinnamomon (κιννάμωμον); according to Herodot the word comes from Hebrew; *venter, ventris* belly (thamnolaea, mocking cliff-chat, 306, 958) F. de Lafresnaye, 1836.

cinnamomeus L. cinnamon-coloured; *cinnamomum* cinnamon; Gr. *kinnamomon (κιννάμωμον);* according to Herodot the word comes from Hebrew; (anthus, african pipit, 350, 1103, E. Rüppel, 1840) (cisticola, pale-crowned cisticola, 330, 841, L. J. P. Vieillot, 1817).

cinnyricinclus Gr. genus cinnyris & kinglos; *kinnuris small bird mentioned by Hesychius, not further identified* (Jobling, 2010, pp. 108); *kinglos (κίγκλος)* a bird mentioned by many ancient Greeks, like a wryneck but Sundevall believes it refers to either *Tringa subarquata* or *T. Alpine*; there is an ancient Gr. saying *poorer than a kinglos* (πτωχότερος κίγκλου) because they believed this bird had no nest of its own (55).

cinnyris Gr. *kinnuris small bird mentioned by Hesychius, not further identified* (Jobling, 2010, pp. 108) (56).

circaetus Gr. harrier-eagle; *kirkos (κίρκος)* hawk, harrier; *aetos (ἀετός)* eagle (40).

circus Gr. harrier; *kirkos (κίρκος)* hawk, harrier; quite a few birds can be found by that name in the writings of ancient Greeks such as Falco palumbarius, F. Pygargus, F. cyaneus or F. nisus; the first meaning was of an unidendified stone (Pliny) the L. words circus, circum, circa all indicate something in a circle and that's probably how the bird got its name from the circles it forms when flying (40).

cirrocephalus Gr. grey-headed ; *kirrhos (κιρρός)* tawny, yellow; *cephale (κεφαλή* ancient Gr.; *κεφάλι* modern Gr.) head (chroicocephalus, grey-headed gull, 184, 443 (larus)) L. J. P. Vieillot, 1818.

cisticola Gr. &. L. small shrub dweller; Gr. *kisthos (κίσθος* or *κισθός)* small shrub with flowers (L. cistus); L. *colere* to dwell, to inhabit (52).

citreola L. small citrine, yellow; *citrus* citrus tree, citron tree; *citreus* of citrus wood; came from Gr. *kedros (κέδρος)* cedar via the Etruscans (motacilla, citrine wagtail, 48, 1094) P. S. Pallas, 1776.

citrinipecta/us *L.* yellow-breasted; *citrine,* yellow; *citrus citrus* tree, citron tree; *citreus* of citrus wood; came from Gr. *kedros (κέδρος) cedar via the Etruscans;* pectus, *pectoris* breast, chest, heart, soul, spirit (crithagra, lemon-breasted canary, 406, 1122) P. Clancey & Lawson, 1960.

clamator L. shouter, bawler, noisy; *clamator, clamatoris* bawler, shouter (bad orator); *clamare* to shout, to cry, accompany with shouts; *clamor, -oris* sound, noise, uproar (31).

clamosus L. shouter, bawler, noisy; *clamosus* noisy; *clamare* to shout, to cry, accompany with shouts; *clamor, -oris* sound, noise, uproar (cuculus, black cuckoo, 214, 206) J. Latham, 1801.

clanga Gr. eagle; *klangazo (κλαγγάζω)* sound of hawks or cranes; L. *clangere* to echo, to resound (aquila, greater spotted eagle, 94, 1141) P. S. Pallas, 1811.

clara L. bright, distinct; *clarus, clara* clear, bright, distinct,

illustrious; Eng. clear, clarity (motacilla, mountain wagtail, 348, 1095) R. B. Sharpe, 1908.

clypeata L. shield-bearing; *clypeus* shield, disk of sun, vault of sky; *clype-are* to arm with a shield or protection (anas, northern shoveler, 82, 110) C. Linnaeus, 1758.

coccopygia Gr. red-rumped; *kokkos (κόκκος)* pip; *kokkino (κόκκινο)* red; *puge (πυγή)* rump (57).

codrigtoni after Robert Edward *Codrington* (1869-1908), the Governor of Northern Rhodesia (now Zambia) between 1898 and 1907; he wrote *A journey from Fort Jameson to Old Chitambo and the Tanganyika Plateau* and *A Voyage on Lake Tanganyika* among many articles for the Geographical Journal (vidua, twinspot indigobird, 394, 1080) S. A. Neave, 1907.

coelebs L. single, unmarried; *caelebs* or *coelebs, -libis* single, unmarried; *refers to single-sex flocks formed by this species* (Roberts;) *Linnaeus remarked that hen Chaffinches wintered south to Holland leaving the cocks to lead a bachelor existence* (Jobling, 2010, pp. 112) (fringilla, common chaffinch, 410, 1115) C. Linnaeus, 1758.

colius Gr. jackdaw, jay or sheath, scabbard; *koloios (κόλοιος)* jackdaw, jay, magpie or *koleos (κολεός)* scabbard, sheath with reference to the long tail (Roberts) (colius, white-backed mousebird, 32, 196) C. Linnaeus, 1766.

collaris L. collared; *collare, -is* collar, neckband, chain for neck; *collum* neck, throat; Eng. collar (hedydipna, collared sunbird, 374, 986, L. J. P. Vieillot, 1818) (lanius, common fiscal, 358, 728, C. Linnaeus, 1766).

collurio Gr. a thrush-like bird mentioned by Aristotle; *kollyrion (κολλυρίων)* probably *turdus pilaris* (lanius, red-backed shrike, 358, 725) C. Linnaeus, 1758.

columba L. pigeon, dove; *columba* pigeon, dove; Gr. *kolymvis,-idos (κολυμβίς, -ίδος)* a bird from the west, probably the wild goose, mentioned by Aristophanes; *kolymvos (κόλυμβος)* swimmer, diver (33).

comeri after George <u>Comer</u> (1858-1937), an American whaling captain, polar explorer, ethnologist and cartographer,

author and photographer who made 14 Arctic and 3 Antarctic voyages (gallinula, gough moorhen, 414,) J. A. Allen, 1892.

communis L. common; *communis* common, ordinary, public, sociable, vulgar, brutal; Eng. common, communism (sylvia, common whitethroat, 314, 819) J. Latham, 1787.

concolor L. of the same colour; *concolor, -oris* of the same colour, matching, of uniform colour (corythaixoides, grey go-away-bird, 210, 249, A. Smith, 1833) (falco, sooty falcon, 120, 553, J. C. Temminck, 1825).

conirostris Gr. & L. cone-billed; Gr. *konos (κῶνος)* cone; L. *conus, coni* cone; *rostrum,-i* bill, beak, curved bow of ship (spizocorys, pink-billed lark, 270, 892) C. J. Sundevall, 1850.

conspicillata L. spectacled (with obvious eye markings); *conspicillum* lookout post, eyeglass, binoculars; *conspicere* observe, see, witness, watch; Eng. conspicuous (procellaria, spectacled petrel, 38, 669) J. Gould, 1844.

coprotheres Gr. dung hunter; *kopros (κόπρος)* dung, faeces;

thera *(θήρα)* hunting wild animals; *therao (θηράω)* to hunt wild animals; the Greek word for hunting is also in the scientific names of lion, leopard etc (pan-thera) and the common name of pan-ther; it means hunting everything (gyps, cape vulture, 86, 489) J. R. Forster, 1798.

coqui probably onomatopoeic for the sound of the bird's call; the same is true for a family of frogs in Puerto Rico; it has been suggested that the bird was named after Mr Coqui, a friend of A. Smith and a well known figure of the eastern frontier of the Cape Colony (peliperdix, coqui francolin, 128, 62) A. Smith, 1836.

coracias Gr. jackdaw, black like a raven; *korax, korakos (κόραξ, κόρακος)* crow, raven; probably refers to crow-like calls; *korakias,- ou (κορακίας, -ου)* a kind of jackdaw; in gr. mythology the crow was white but in at least two different myths it brought bad news to two gods; one was Athena and the other Apollo; in both cases the messenger was punished not to be white anymore (30).

coracina Gr. like a raven, black like a raven; *korakinos (κοράκινος)* like a raven, black like a raven; *korax, korakos (κόραξ, κόρακος)* crow, raven (49).

coronatus Gr. crowned; *korone* (Dorian Gr. *korona*) *(κορώνη, κορώνα)* crown; Eng. <u>coron</u>ation (phalacrocorax, crowned cormorant, 56, 573, J. A. Wahlberg, 1855) (stephanoaetus, african crowned eagle, 96, 541, C. Linnaeus, 1766) (vanellus, crowned lapwing, 156, 417, P. Boddaert, 1783).

corruscus L. shining, bright; *coruscus* brilliant, flashing, twinkling, vibrating, waving; *coruscare* to shine, to shake; Eng. coruscate (lamprotornis, black-bellied starling, 366, 962, A. Von Nordmann, 1835).

corvinella L. a small crow; *corvus* crow, raven; Gr. *korax, korakos (κόραξ, κόρακος)* crow, raven (48).

corvus L. crow, raven; *corvus* crow, raven; Gr. *korax, korakos (κόραξ, κόρακος)* crow, raven (48).

coryphoeus Gr. leader, top; a name of Artemis, goddess of hunting (Diana of the Romans); *Levaillant* believed this bird to be as melodious as the Common

Nightingale (Jobling, 2010, pp. 119); in drama the *korypheos (κορυφαῖος)* is the leader of the chorus and speaks to the actors (cercotrichas, karoo scrub-robin, 308, 942) L. J. P. Vieillot, 1817.

corythaix Gr. shaking the crest; *korythaix (κορυθάϊξ)* waving the helmet (Homer's Iliad, X 123); *korys, korythos (κόρυς, κόρυθος)* helmet (usually made of copper); *aisso (αἴσσω)* to move rapidly, to shake (tauraco, knysna turaco, 210, 246) J. G. Wagler, 1827.

corythaixoides Gr. like corythaix; shaking the crest; *korythaix (κορυθάϊξ)* waving the helmet (Homer's Iliad, X 123); *korys, korythos (κόρυς, κόρυθος)* helmet (usually made of copper); *aisso (αἴσσω)* to move rapidly, to shake; *-oides -οειδές* resembling (32).

cossypha Gr. blackbird, thrush; *kossyphos (κόσσυφος) (kotsyphas (κότσυφας)* in modern Gr.) blackbird, thrush and specifically the European blackbird *turdus merula* (54).

coturnix L. quail; *coturnix, coturnicis* quail (26) (coturnix, common quail, 132, 75) C. Linnaeus, 1758.

crassirostris L. thick-billed; *crassus* thick, deep, heavy, rude, rough, harsh; *rostrum, -i* bill, beak, curved bow of ship (vanellus, long-toed lapwing, 158, 407) G. Hartlaub, 1855.

creatophora Gr. flesh carrier; *kreas, -atos (κρέας, -ατος)* meat; *fero (φέρω)* to carry (55).

crecopsis Gr. appearing like genus *crex;* a short legged bird with long and serrated beak; *krex krekos (κρέξ, κρεκός)* in Aristophanes' Birds (1138); *kreko (κρέκω)* onomatopoeic, usually of a string/chord; *opsis (ὄψις)* appearance or face (35).

crenatus L. notched; *crena, crenae* notch, serration, slash (anthus, African rock-pipit, 352, 1102) O. Finsch & G. Hartlaub, 1870.

crex Gr. a short legged bird with long and serrated beak; *krex krekos (κρέξ, κρεκός)* in Aristophanes' Birds (1138); *kreko (κρέκω)* onomatopoeic, usually of a string/chord (35) (crex, corn crake, 138, 325) C. Linnaeus, 1758.

cristata/cristatus L. crested, tufted, plumed; *crista, -ae* crest, plume; *crinis* hair, comet's tail (alcedo, malachite kingfisher, 234, 174, P.S. Pallas, 1764) (fulica, red-knobbed coot, 134, 336, J. F. Gmelin, 1789) (pavo, common peacock, 124, 79, C. Linnaeus, 1758) (podiceps, great crested grebe, 60, 561, C. Linnaeus, 1758).

crithagra Gr. barley hunting; *krithe (κριθή)* barley; *agra (ἄγρα)* hunting; *Agra* a name for the goddess of hunting, Artemis (59).

croceus Gr. yellow, golden-yellow; *krokos (κρόκος)* crocus, saffron, yolk; Hebrew *karkom;* Arabic *kurkum;* Akkadian *kurkanu;* L. *crocus* or *crocum* is a loan from Gr. (macronyx, yellow-throated longclaw, 356, 1097) L. J. P. Vieillot, 1816.

crumeniferus L. &. Gr. carrying a pouch; L. *crumena* a pouch around the neck; Gr. *fero (φέρω)* to carry; marabou derives from Arabic *murabit* hermit; Fr. *marabout;* Portuguese *marabuto* (leptoptilos, marabou stork, 72, 626) R. P. Lesson, 1831.

cryptillas Gr. hidden thrush; *kryptos (κρυπτός)* hidden, secret, clandestine; *krypto (κρύπτω)* to hide, cover up; *illas,*

illados (ἰλλάς, ἰλλάδος) from *ilias (ἰλιάς)* a type of thrush (51).

cryptospiza Gr. hidden finch; *kryptos (κρυπτός)* hidden, secret, clandestine; *krypto (κρύπτω)* to hide, cover up; *spiza (σπίζα)* finch; *spizo (σπίζω)* to sing like a little bird (57).

cryptoxanthus Gr. hidden yellow or blonde; *refers to yellow axillaries, visible only in flight* (Roberts); *kryptos (κρυπτός)* hidden, secret, clandestine; *krypto (κρύπτω)* to hide, cover up; *xanthos (ξανθός)* blond, yellow, fair, the colour of mature wheat (poicephalus, brown-headed parrot, 206, 224) W. Peters, 1854.

cubla Jobling (2010, pp. 124) reports that it derives from Fr. *cul blanc* white rump; Roberts though claims *'it is named by Le Vaiilant; of Bantu or Hottentot origin and it is onomatopoeic and the 'c' is pronounced with a click'* (dryoscopus, black-backed puffback, 364, 690) G. Shaw, 1809.

cucullata /cucullatus L. hooded; *cucullus* hood, cap, cowl, cover for the head (hirundo, greater striped swallow, 276, 755, P. Boddaert, 1783) (ploceus, village weaver, 384, 1018, S. Müller, 1776) (spermestes, bronze manikin, 404, 1065, W. J. Swainson, 1837).

cuculoides L. & Gr. resembling a cuckoo; *cuculus* cuckoo, ninny, fool, cuckold, bastard; - *oides (οειδές)* resembling (aviceda, African cuckoo-hawk114, 474) W. J. Swainson, 1837.

cuculus L. cuckoo; *cuculus* cuckoo, ninny, fool, cuckold, bastard; Eng. cuckoo; Fr. coucou; Ger. Kuckuck; Sp. cuco (31).

cupreicaudus L. coppery tail; *referring to violet sheen on retrices* (Roberts); *cuprum* copper; *cauda* tail (centropus, coppery-tailed coucal, 218, 217) A. Reichenow, 1896.

cupreus L. coppery; *cuprum* copper; from Cyprus *(Κύπρος)* Eng. copper; Fr. cuivre; Ger. Kupfer; Sp. cobre; It. cupro (chrysococcyx, african emerald cuckoo 216, 213, G. Shaw, 1792) (cinnyris, copper sunbird, 378, 995, G. Shaw, 1811).

cursorius L. courier, runner; *currere* run, trot, gallop, hurry, hasten, travel (38).

curvirostris L. curved-bill; *curvare* to bend, to curve; *rostrum,-i* bill, beak, curved bow of ship (certhilauda, cape long-billed lark, 262, 879) J. Hermann, 1783.

cuvierii after Georges-Frédéric *Cuvier* (1773-1838), a French zoologist and palaeontologist and younger brother of Georges Cuvier, sometimes referred to as the "Father of paleontology"; he was elected as a foreign member of the Royal Society in 1835; he is mentioned in Charles Darwin's *on the Origin of Species* and in *Moby-Dick;* he was the head keeper of the menagerie at the Museum d'Histoire Naturelle in Paris from 1804 to his death (falco, african hobby, 118, 555) A. Smith, 1830.

cyanomelas Gr. blue black; *kyanos (κυανός)* dark blue; *melas, melanos (μέλας, μέλανος)* black; Eng. *cyan*-ide, cyan-osis; *mela*nine; (rhinopomastus, common scimitarbill, 248, 165, L. J. P. Vieillot, 1819) (trochocercus, blue-mantled crested-flycatcher, 342, 685, L. J. P. Vieillot, 1818).

cyanomitra Gr. blue headband; *kyanos (κυανός)* dark blue; *mitra (μίτρα)* head-band, diadem (56).

cypsiurus Gr. swallow-tailed; *kypselos (κύψελος)* swallow (hirundo apus); *oura (οὐρά)* tail; the word *kypselos (κύψελος)* a round shaped pot, describes the shape of the nest that only *hirundo riparia* builds (32).

D

dabbenena after Roberto *Dabbene* (1864-1938), an Italian-Argentine ornithologist; he moved from Italy to Argentina where he studied birds for over 40 years and wrote a number of books about them (diomedea, tristan albatross, 20, 643) G. Mathews, 1929.

dactylatra Gr. and L. Black fingers referring to its black primaries; Gr. daktyla (δάκτυλα) fingers and L. *ater* black (sula, masked booby, 52, 1142) R-P. Lesson, 1831.

damarensis from Damaraland; an area in north-central Namibia, inhabited by the Damaras who call them shelves Daman, meaning black people; the last -n is simply the plural ending of Khoekhoe, the language the Damaras speak (phoeniculus, violet wood-hoopoe, 248, 164,

W. R. Ogilvie-Grant, 1901) (tockus, damara hornbill, 246, 151, Shelley, 1888).

daption it was suggested that its name is an anagramm of *pintado* Spanish or Portuguese for painted but it probably derives from Ancient Greek and it means 'little devourer' *daptes (δάπτης)* devourer, blood drinker; *dapto (δάπτω)* to devour (46).

daurica after Dauria (Даурия), a mountainous region beyond Lake Baikal in Russia; named after the Daur or Daguur people, a Mongolic-speaking people (hirundo, red-rumped swallow, 274, 759) E. G. Laxman, 1769.

decipiens L. deceiving; *decipere* to cheat, to ensnare, to deceive; according to Roberts it's called that because *'it closely resembles other collared doves'* (streptopelia, african mourning dove, 202, 283) G. Hartlaub & O. Finsch, 1870.

delegorguei after Louis Adolphe Joseph *Delegorgue* (1814-1850), a French traveller, hunter, naturalist and collector in South Africa; he left his collections to the British Natural History Museum; his adventures were published in 1847 as *Travels in Southern Africa;* he may have collected with J. A. Wahlberg (columba, eastern bronze-naped pigeon, 200, 279, A. Delegorgue 1847) (coturnix, harlequin quail, 132, A. Delegorgue, 1847).

delichon Gr. anagram of *chelidon (χελιδών)* swallow; *khlidon, khlidonos (χλίδων, χλίδωνος)* a jewel for the arms, neck or legs (49).

demersus L. plunging, sinking; *demergere* to plunge, to sink, to submerge, to dip (spheniscus, african penguin, 16, 631) C. Linnaeus, 1758.

dendrocygna Gr. tree swan; *dendron, dentro (δένδρον and δέντρο* in modern Gr.)* tree; *cygnos (κύκνος)* swan (26).

dendroperdix Gr. tree partridge; *dendron, dentro (δένδρον and δέντρο* in modern Gr.)* tree; *perdix (πέρδιξ, πέρδικα* in modern Gr.) partridge; *perdomai (πέρδομαι)* to fart, to break wind; refers to the sound of the bird's wings when alarmed!(26).

dendropicos Gr. tree-woodpecker; *dendron, dentro (δένδρον* and *δέντρο* in modern Gr.) tree; *picos (πίκος)* woodpecker; in Roman mythology Picus was the first king of Latium, son of Saturnus; he was turned into a woodpecker by Circe, the witch, after rejecting her amorous proposals; his wife was turned into a *pica* a magpie; another version attributes skills of interpretation of bird omens to Picus and his transformation into a bird is justified (28).

denhami after Dixon *Denham* (1786-1828), an English lieutenant-colonel, explorer of many parts of Africa, an illustrator and Governor-General of Sierra Leone where he died of 'african fever', probably malaria; he wrote *Narrative of Travels and Discoveries in Northern and Central Africa* in 1826 (neotis, denham's bustard, 144, 291) J. G. Children & N. A. Vigors, 1826.

desolata L. desolated, forsaken; *desolare* to abandon; maybe after Desolation island which was the name Captain Cook used for Kerguelen island or the desolate part of the Antarctic where they live (pachyptila, antarctic prion, 34, 664) J. F. Gmelin, 1789.

dichroa Gr. two-coloured; dichroos & *dichrous (δίχροος*

& δίχρους) two coloured; di *(δύο) two; chroa (χρόα)* colour, complexion (cossypha, chorister robin-chat, 310, 934) J. F. Gmelin, 1789.

dickinsoni after Dr John <u>Dickinson</u> (1832-1864), *an English physician and missionary who joined Livingston but died of blackwater fever in Nyasaland (now Malawi). He collected the type specimen of the kestrel himself* (Beolens & Watkins, 2003, pp. 105) (falco, dickinson's kestrel, 120, 549) P. L. Sclater, 1864.

dicrurus Gr. fork-tailed; dicroos or dicrus *(δίκροος or δίκρους)* forked, having two teeth; it is used for the double hooves of animals or a snake's tongue; *oura (ουρά)* tail (47).

diffusus L. diffuse, extensive; *diffundere* to spread out, pour out/forth, (passer, southern grey-headed sparrow, 380, 1086) A. Smith, 1836.

dimidiata L. divided; *dis-* apart (s is lost before m); *medius* middle, *dimidiata* halved, divided; *dimidiare* to divide; probably refers to incomplete throat band (Roberts, 2009, pp. 754) (hirundo, pearl-breasted

swallow, 278, 754) C. J. Sundevall, 1850.

diomedea Gr. after Diomedes, a very important Greek hero of the Iliad, King of Argos, a traveller and founder of many cities in Italy; *Diomedes (Διομήδης)* the mind of Zeus, advised by Zeus; *Dias (Δίας)* Zeus; *medos (μῆδος)* mind, thinking; the name of the birds derives from various myths; either because his companions turned to birds when he died or because albatrosses gathered and started singing their song on the hero's death of old age (calonectris, cory's shearwater, 40, 670) G. A. Scopoli, 1769.

domesticus L. belonging to the house, familiar, domestic; *domus* house, home, homeland, country, family, school; from Gr. *domos (δόμος)* home, room (passer, house sparrow, 380, 1082) C. Linnaeus, 1758.

dominica after Santo Domingo; L. belonging to lord/master; Santo Domingo was the first Spanish colony in the Carribean and the second largest island of the carribean after Cuba; the island was originally named Insula Hispana by C. Columbus, shortened Española by Bartolomé de las Casas; later it was called Santo Domingo, St. Domingue and San Domingo; the island is divided into two sovereign states, the Dominican republic and Haiti; today the whole island is known by the Latin translation of its original name *Hispaniola* (pluvialis, american golden plover, 160, 394) P. L. S. Müller, 1776.

dominicanus L. refers to the black and white plumage which resembles the habits or robes of the *Dominican* friars; the Dominican Order was founded by the Spanish priest Dominic de Guzman (1170-1221), now Saint Dominic, the patron saint of astronomers (larus, kelp gull, 188, 439) M. Lichtenstein, 1823.

dougallii after Dr Peter Mc*Dougall* (1777-1814), a Scottish physician, naturalist and collector; Montagu described the bird he was sent by Mc Dougall, among other birds (sterna, roseate tern, 192, 456) G. Montagu, 1813.

dromas Gr. a runner; *dromas (δρομάς)* runner, fast spinning circle, running around the streets (prostitute); *dromos* (δρόμος) running competition; in modern Gr. it means road (38).

dryoscopus Gr. a watcher from trees; *drys (δρῦς)* meant all trees but later it meant only the oak tree; *scopeo* (σκοπέω) to watch (47).

dubius L. doubtful, uncertain; Jobling reports that Sonnerat in 1776 wasn't sure whether the bird was a separate species or just a separable example of the ringed plover, *charadrius hiaticula*, whose plumage had been subtly altered (2010, pp. 141) (charadrius, little ringed plover, 152, 397) G. A. Scopoli, 1786.

E

ecaudatus L. lacking tail; *ex-* lacking; *cauda* tail; its common name 'bateleur' is French for 'tightrope walker' and refers to the bird's aerial acrobatics (terathopius, bateleur, 90, 498) F. M. Daudin, 1800.

edouardi after Jean Baptiste *Edouard* Verreaux (1810-1868), French naturalist, collector and dealer who worked at the Cape, nephew of P. A. Delalande (guttera, crested guineafowl, 124, 81) G. Hartlaub, 1867.

egregia L. singular or excellent; *egregia* singular, distinguished, exceptional, extraordinary, illustrious, outstanding; *ex + grex; grex, -gis* pack, herd (crecopsis, african crake, 138, 324) W. Peters, 1854.

egretta from French *aigrette* an egret or small heron; Fr. *aigrette* egret, heron, tuft of very thin feathers on the head of the bird, tuft on the hat of a soldier (42)

elanus Gr. kite (39)

elegans L. elegant; *elegans, elegantis* elegant, fine, handsome, tasteful; *eligere* to choose, select with care; *ex + lego;* the meaning of elegant emerged in classical L.; the original meaning was that of fastidious and it showed reproach (sarothrura, buff-spotted flufftail, 140, 315, A. Smith, 1839) (sterna, elegant tern, 190, W. Gambel, 1849).

eleonorae after *Eleanor* of Arborea (1347-1404), *iuyghissa* (female judge), warrior princess and Sardinia's most renowned heroine, as she liberated the island from the Crown of Aragon; she passed a law to protect birds of prey although some might say that this was to keep them for the aristocracy; Alberto Ferrero Della Marmora named the bird after her and Gené described it (Beolens & Watkins, 2003, pp. 117) (falco, eleonora's falcon, 118, 553) G. Gené, 1839.

elisabeth named by German ornithologist Erwin Stresemann after his first wife *Elisabeth* Deniger (lamprotornis, miombo blue-eared starling, 366, 965) E. Stresseman, 1924.

elminia after Elmina, a town on the south coast of Ghana; it was the first European settlement in West Africa; it was called *Anomansah* (the perpetual drink) before the Portuguese captured it; then the Dutch came, followed by the British (50).

emberiza old German name *Embritz* for a bunting (Jobling, 2010, pp. 145) or Gr. bunting (59).

ephippiorhynchus Gr. saddle-billed; *epi (ἐπί)* on; *hippos (ἵππος)* horse; *ephippos* mounted, on horseback; *rynchos* (ρύγχος) *bill, beak, snout* (44).

episcopus Gr. bishop; *episcopos (ἐπίσκοπος)* bishop, referring to black cap or purple or blue plumage (Jobling, 2010, pp. 147);

older meaning was guardian, watcher (ciconia, wooly-necked stork, 72, 622) P. Boddaert, 1783.

epomophora Gr. carrying on the shoulder; *epi (ἐπί)* on; *omos (ὦμος)* shoulder; *fero (φέρω)* to bring to carry; *epomis, epomidos (ἐπωμίς, ἐπωμίδος)* ancient Gr. shoulder, modern Gr. epaulet, shoulder strap (diomedea, southern royal albatross, 22, 643) R. Lesson, 1825.

epops Gr. hoopoe; *epops, epopos (ἔποψ, ἔποπος)* hoopoe; it is onomatopoeic, imitating the bird's voice although it has been suggested that it derives from *epoptes (ἐπόπτης)* guard, all watching; especially for gods ie Poseidon, the Sun etc.; Tereas, the king of the imaginary bird state of Aristophanes comedy *Birds (Ornithes Ὄρνιθες)* is a hoopoe, called *Epops* (upupa (now upupa africana), african hoopoe, 248, 160) J. M. Bechstein, 1811.

eremita Gr. hermit; *eremites (ἐρημίτης)* hermit; *eremos (ἔρημος)* desert; Chatham albatross is so called because it only breeds on the Pyramid, a rock stack in the Chatham Islands of New Zealand (Rekohu, meaning 'misty sun' in Maori)

(nesocichla, tristan thrush, 414, C. Linnaeus, 1758) (thalassarche, chatham albatross, 24, 647, R. C. Murphy, 1930).

eremomela Gr. desert or wilderness song; *eremos (ἔρημος)* desert; *melos (μέλος)* song, melody, sound, music (51).

eremopterix Gr. desert wing or desert bird; *eremos (ἔρημος)* desert; *pteryx, pterygos (πτέρυξ, πτέρυγος)* wing (53).

erythrocephala Gr. red headed; *erythros (ἐρυθρός)* red; *cephale (κεφαλή* ancient Gr.; *κεφάλι* modern Gr.) head; *Erythrea* or *Eritrea* derives from the Gr. word for red from the *Red sea* (amadina, red-headed finch, 404, 1041) C. Linnaeus, 1758.

erythrocercus Gr. red tail; *erythros (ἐρυθρός)* red; cercos *(κέρκος)* animal tail (50)

erythronotos Gr. red backed; *erythros (ἐρυθρός)* red; *noton* or *notos (νῶτον* or *νῶτος)* the back of humans and vertebrate animals (estrilda, black-faced waxbill, 396, 1047) L. J. P. Vieillot, 1847.

erythrophthalma Gr. red-eyed; *erythros (ἐρυθρός)* red;

ophthalmos (ὀφθαλμός) eye; Eng. ophthalmologist (netta, southern pochard, 80, 116) Prince Maximilian of Wied-Neuwied, 1832-33.

erythrops Gr. red-faced; erythros (ἐρυθρός) red; ops (ὤψ) face, eye; cyclops means circular eye; neither bird with this name has red eyes (cisticola, red-faced cisticola, 334, 824, G. Hartlaub, 1857) (quelea, red-headed quelea, 388, 1024, G. Hartlaub, 1848).

erythropterus Gr. red-winged; erythros (ἐρυθρός) red; pteron (πτερόν) or ftero (φτερό) in modern Gr. wing (heliolais, red-winged warbler, 336, 848) W. Jardine, 1849.

erythropus Gr. red-legged or red-footed; erythros (ἐρυθρός) red; pous, podos (πούς, ποδός) foot, leg (tringa, spotted redshank, 168, 351) P. S. Pallas, 1764.

e r y t h r o r y n c h a / erythorhynchus Gr. red-billed; erythros (ἐρυθρός) red; rhynchos (ρύγχος) bill or snout; in comedy a human face (anas, red-billed teal, 84, 111, J. F. Gmelin, 1789) (buphagus, red-billed oxpecker, 370, 973, E. Smith-Stanley,

1814) (tockus, southern red-billed hornbill, 246, 149, C. J. Temminck, 1823).

estrilda it has been suggested that the name derives from Dutch or German and it is a term for a waxbill (Jobling, 2010, pp. 151) or that it derives from Gr. astron (ἄστρον) star ie L. astrum (Roberts, 2009) (57).

eudyptes Gr. good diver; eu (εὖ) good, fine; dyptes (δύπτης) diver; dypto (δύπτω) to dive (44).

eudyptula Gr. good diver; diminutive of eudyptes; eu (εὖ) good, fine; dyptes (δύπτης) diver; dypto (δύπτω) to dive.

euplectes Gr. good weaver; eu (εὖ) good, fine; plectes (πλέκτης) weaver; pleco (πλέκω) to weave; if it referred to the nests it would be euplektos (εὔπλεκτος) (57).

eupodotis Gr. good foot (swift) bustard; eu (εὖ) good, fine; pous, podos (πούς, ποδός) foot or leg; otis (ὠτίς) bustard (34).

eurocephalus Gr. broad-headed; eyrus (εὐρύς) broad, wide; cephale (κεφαλή ancient Gr.; κεφάλι modern Gr.) head (48).

europeus Gr. of Europe or European; three different etymologies have been suggested. 1. large eyes, *eurys (εὐρύς)* wide + ops *(ὤψ)* eye; 2. *europos (εὐρωπός)* wide, *europis (εὐρωπίς)* homeland; 3. *euros (εὐρώς)* mould, mildew; one of the five continents; not possible to connect mythological Europe to the name of the continent; she was the daughter of Agenor and Zeus's mistress and mother to Sarpedon, Rhadamanthys and Minos; Zeus seduced her by transforming himself into a white bull (caprimulgus, european nightjar, 224, 273) C. Linnaeus, 1758.

euryptila Gr. broad-feathered; *eyrus (εὐρύς)* broad, wide; *ptilon (πτίλον)* feather (52).

eurystomus Gr. broad mouth, wide-mouthed; *eyrus (εὐρύς)* broad, wide; *stoma (στόμα)* mouth (30).

explorator L. explorer, spy, scout; *explorare* to investigate, to ascertain, to search out (monticola, sentinel rock-thrush, 300, 898) L. J. P. Vieillot, 1818.

exulans L. living as an exile or wandering; *exulans* or *exsul* exile or wander; *exulare* or exsulare live in exile, be banished, be a stranger (diomedea, wandering albatross, 20. 641) C. Linnaeus, 1758.

F

falcinellus L. sickle; diminutive of *falx, falcis* sickle, scythe, curved blade, pruning knife; Gr. *falkis (φάλκης)* burnt wood for shipbuilding; refers to the curved bill of the ibis and the decurved at tip bill of the sandpiper (limicola, broad-billed sandpiper, 162, 375, E. Pontoppidan, 1763) (plegadis, glossy ibis, 76, 607, C. Linnaeus, 1766).

falco L. falcon; probably from *falx, falcis* sickle, scythe, curved blade, pruning knife; refers to the birds' talons or legs or beaks or the shape of their spread wings (Portuguese *falcao*, Italian *falcone*, German *falke*, Dutch *valk*) (41).

fallax L. deceptive, false; *fallere* to deceive, to disappoint, cheat, beguile, be mistaken; it was thus named as it was not described until 1950 and its breeding site was only found in 2000; its common name commemorates

Christian *Jouanin* (1925-), a French ornithologist and expert on Petrels; he described the bird as different to Bonaparte's (bulweria, jouanin's petrel, 44, 667) C. Jouanin, 1955.

familiaris L. familiar, friendly, domestic, private, belonging to a family, of a household; L. *familia* included relatives and servants; *famulus* slave, puppet, stooge (cercomela, familiar chat, 302, 955) Wilkes, 1817 or Stephens, 1826.

famosa L. famous, renowned, talked of; *fama* fame, talk, rumour, reputation, glory, praise (nectarinia, malachite sunbird, 372, 985) C. Linnaeus, 1766.

fasciata L. banded, striped; *fascia* band, strip, ribbon, streak; *fascism* derives from this word; *fascis* was the symbol of power and it was a band of rods with an axe in the middle; Mussolini adopted the symbol and the name for his party in 1919 (amadina, cut-throat finch, 404, 1042). J.F. Gmelin, 1789.

fasciinucha L. banded nape; *fascia* band, strip, ribbon, streak; *nucha* nape, back of neck from Arabic *nukha* (نُخَاع) marrow; its common name is from Taita hills in south eastern Kenya where the bird was first discovered (falco, taita falcon, 116, 559) A. Reichenow & O. R. Neumann, 1895.

fasciolata/fasciolatus L. barred, banded; *fasciola* diminutive of *fascia* band, strip, ribbon, streak, swaddling-band (calamonastes, barred wren-warbler, 322, 858, A. Smith, 1847) (circaetus, southern banded snake-eagle, 92, 496, J. J. Kaup, 1850) (mirafra, eastern clapper lark, 264, 866, C. J. Sundevall, 1850.)

ferruginea /ferrugineus L. rusty-coloured. *ferrum,-i* iron, tool, weapon; *ferrugo,-inis* rust; rust is an iron oxide formed by the reaction between iron and oxygen; rust consists of $Fe_2O_3nH_2O$ hydrated iron oxides and (FeO (OH), Fe (OH) 3 iron oxide-hydroxide (calidris, curlew sandpiper, 162, 373, E. Pontoppidan, 1763) (laniarius, southern boubou, 360, 697, J. F. Gmelin, 1788).

ficedula L. fig-pecker, fig-eater; *ficus* fig (Roberts claims it's erroneous as birds *are attracted by insects visiting figs*) (54).

flava L. yellow; *flavus, flava* yellow, gold, blonde, flaxen; like *fulvus*, flavus has the meaning of shine like the sun (campephaga, black cuckooshrike, 284, 733, L. J. P. Vieillot, 1817) (motacilla, yellow wagtail, 348, 1092, C. Linnaeus, 1758).

flavicans L. yellowish, golden-yellowish; *flavus* yellow, gold, blonde, flaxen; like *fulvus*, flavus has the meaning of shine like the sun (prinia, black-chested prinia, 338, 844) L. J. P. Vieillot, 1820.

flavida L. yellowish, pale yellow; *flavus, flava* yellow, gold, blonde, flaxen (apalis, yellow-breasted apalis, 326, 852) H. E. Strickland, 1853.

flavigaster L & Gr. gellow belly; *flavus* (L) yellow, gold, blonde, flaxen; Gr. g*aster, gasteros* (γαστήρ, γαστέρος) belly, stomach, womb; Eng. *gastr*onomy, *gastr*itis (hyliota, yellow-bellied hyliota, 344, 808) W. J. Swainson, 1837.

flavipes L. yellow-footed; *flavus* yellow, gold, blonde, flaxen; *pes, pedis* foot (tringa, lesser yellowlegs, 168, 356) J. F. Gmelin, 1789.

flavirostra/flavirostris L. yellow or golden billed; *flavus* yellow,

gold, blonde, flaxen; *rostrum* bill (amaurornis, black crake, 136, 326, W. J. Swainson, 1837) (rynchops, african skimmer, 188, 437, L. J. P. Vieillot, 1816).

flaviventris L. yellow belly; *flavus* yellow, gold, blonde, flaxen; *venter, ventris* belly, stomach (chlorocichla, yellow-bellied greenbul, 296, 772, A. Smith, 1834) (crithagra, yellow canary, 406, 1124, W. J. Swainson, 1828) (emberiza, golden-breasted bunting, 412, 1136, J. F. Stephens, 1815).

flavostriatus L. yellow-streaked; *flavus* yellow, gold, blonde, flaxen; *striatus* striated; *striare* to furrow, wrinkle; *stria* furrow, channel (phyllastrephus, yellow-streaked greenbul, 296, 775) R. B. Sharpe, 1876.

fluviatilis L. riverine, of a river; *fluvius* river, stream, running water; *fluere* flow, drip, flood, swim (locustella, river warbler, 320, 791) J. Wolf, 1810.

formicivora L. ant-eating; *formica,-ae* ant; *vorare* devour, swallow. Gr. *vora (βορά)* food esp. of wild animals (myrmecocichla, ant-eating chat, 306, 956) L. J. P. Vieillot or Wilkes, 1817.

forsteri after Johann Reinhold *Forster* (1729-1798); Forster accompanied James Cook on his second voyage; with the *Resolution* they went deeper into Antarctic waters than anyone before; Forster discovered five species of penguins and was probably the first one to see the emperor penguin (aptenodytes, emperor penguin, 18) G. R. Gray, 1844.

fossii after W. *Fosse*, a German collector in Gabon (Roberts, 2009, pp.269) (caprimulgus, square-tailed nightjar, 226, 269) G. Hartlaub, 1857.

fratrum L. of brothers; after Robert B. Woodward (1848-1899) and his brother John DS (1849-1899), Anglican missionaries in Natal, SA; they collected and sent specimens to Sharpe at the British Museum; they wrote *Natal Birds* and it was published just before they died (batis, woodward's batis, 346, 715) G. E. Shelley, 1900.

fregata French *frégate* small, swift vessel, frigatebirds; the name was used in 1738 and it was used by French mariners to describe the bird; C. Columbus encountered those birds and called them forktails, *rabihorcado* in Spanish (*rabiforçado*); Gr. *afraktos* (ἄφρακτος) defenceless; *afraktos nafs* (ἄφρακτος ναῦς) defenceless ship (44).

fregetta diminutive of genus name *Fregata;* French *frégate* small, swift vessel, frigatebirds (45).

frenatus L. bridled; *frenum* bridle, rein, harness; *frenare* to bridle, restrain, brake; referring to face pattern (chaetops, cape rock-jumper, 300, 734) C. J. Temminck, 1826.

fringilla L. chaffinch, finch (59).

fringillaris L. resembling *fringilla*, a chaffinch (spizocorys, botha's lark, 270, 893) C. J. Sundevall, 1850.

fringilloides L. like *fringilla*, a chaffinch; Gr. ending *-oides* resembling (spermestes, magpie mannikin, 404, 1067) F. de Lafresnaye, 1835.

fuelleborni after Dr Friedrich *Fülleborn* (1866-1933), a German physician who specialized in tropical medicine and parasitology; he worked in East Africa for seven years (pseudalethe, white-chested alethe, 310, 909) A. Reichenow, 1900.

fulica L. water-fowl probably a coot; from bird's colour *fuligo* soot, lampblack; (35).

fulicarius L. like a water-fowl probably a coot; *fulica* coot; from bird's colour *fuligo* soot, lampblack (phalaropus, red phalarope, 174, 379) C. Linnaeus, 1758.

fuligula L. dull brown or sooty throat; *fuligo* soot, lampblack; *gula* throat (hirundo, rock martin, 282, 761) M. Lichtenstein, 1842.

fulmarus foul gull; old Norse, *full* foul; *màr* gull, in reference to the smell of their stomach oil which they ejected on hunters who tried to collect them from their nests (46).

fulva L. tawny or yellowish brown; *fulvus, -a* tawny, reddish yellow, yellow, brown, bronze; *fulgere* to shine, to excel (pluvialis, pacific golden plover, 160, 394) J. F. Gmelin, 1789.

fulvicapilla L. tawny hair; *fulvus, -a* tawny, reddish yellow, yellow, brown, bronze; *capillus* hair, hair of head; its common

name is from Afrikaans (cisticola, neddicky, 336, 836) L. J. P. Vieillot, 1817.

funerea L. funereal, dark, of a funeral, fatal; *funereus,-a* or *funebris* deadly, disastrous, of a funeral, of an epitaph; *funus, -eris* funeral, death, corpse, ruin, destruction; obviously in reference to the black colour of the bird (vidua, dusky indigbird, 394, 1078) de Tarragon, 1847.

fusca/fuscus L. dark, dull; *fuscus,-a* dark, swarthy, dusky, husky, hoarse, sunburnt, faint, dim; it is used to describe many different bird colours, mainly dark or dusky shade of many colours; *fuscare* to darken (phoebetria, sooty albatross, 30, 653, C. Hilsenberg, 1822) (larus, lesser black-backed gull, 188, 441, C. Linnaeus, 1758) (cinnyris, dusky sunbird, 374, 996, L. J. P. Vieillot, 1819).

fuscatus L. dark, dull, dusky, sooty; *fuscus,-a* dark, swarthy, dusky, husky, hoarse; *fuscare* to darken (onychoprion, sooty tern, 194, 467 (sterna) C. Linnaeus, 1766.

fuscescens L. blackish, becoming dark or brown; *fuscus,-a* dark, swarthy, dusky, husky, hoarse; *fuscare* to darken (dendropicos, cardinal woodpecker, 256, 135) L. J. P. Vieillot, 1818.

fuscicollis L. dusky-necked; *fuscus,-a* dark, swarthy, dusky, husky, hoarse; *collum* neck, throat, head and neck (calidris, white-rumped sandpiper, 164, 370, L. J. P. Vieillot, 1819) (poicephalus, grey-headed parrot, 206, 222, H. Kuhl, 1820).

G

gabar barred guard; Jobling (2010, pp. 169) suggests *'French origin of homophone garde watchman, guard; barré barred'*; Roberts states *'Khoi origin and the meaning is uncertain'* (melierax, gabar goshawk, 110, 511) F. M. Daudin, 1800.

galactotes Gr. milk (white) resembling, milk-white; *gala (γάλα)* milk; Eng. *gala*xy (cisticola, rufous-winged cisticola, 334, 831) C. J. Temminck, 1821.

galerida L. helmeted or capped; *galerum* cap or hat made of skin worn by soldiers, priests and farmers, wig; *galea* helmet, casque (53).

gallinago L. woodcock, snipe; *gallina* hen; *gallus* rooster, cock (36).

gallinula L. small hen, chicken; *gallina* hen; *gallus* rooster, cock (35).

gallirex L. king cock, referring to crest and red skin around eye; *gallus* cock, rooster; *rex* king (32).

gambensis from Gambia; Gambia is the smallest country in mainland Africa and lies in West Africa; it takes its name from the river that crosses the country; the meaning of the name is not known but Portuguese *cambio* exchange, and local name of *Ba- dimma* river (which means river), have been suggested (plectropterus, spur-winged goose, 78, 95) C. Linnaeus, 1766.

garrodia after Alfred Henry *Garrod* (1846-1879), an English zoologist, whose main interest was bird and ruminant anatomy; he described several of the Challenger expedition specimens (1142).

garrulus L. chattering; *garrulus* talkative, loquatius, chattering, garrulous, betraying secrets; *garrire* chatter, jabber, talk rapidly, talk nonsense (coracias, european roller, 242, 168) C. Linnaeus, 1758.

garzetta Italian name for the little egret; *sgarzetta* in Hungarian (egretta, little egret, 64, 583) C. Linnaeus, 1766.

genei after Carlo Giuseppe Gené (1800-1847), an Italian Professor of zoology and author; he published many papers on zoology but his main interest was entomology (chroicocephalus, slender-billed gull, 184, 447(larus)) Bréme, 1840.

geocolaptes Gr. earth-pecker; *geo (γεω-)* ground, earth; *kolapto (κολάπτω)* to chisel, to peck, to strike (for birds) Eng. geo-graphy, geo-logy (28).

georgicus after South Georgia; the island of South Georgia was claimed for the kingdom of Great Britain by James Cook in 1775 and named 'the Isle of Georgia' after King George III; Gr. *georgia (γεωργία)* agriculture (pelecanoides, south Georgian diving-petrel, 48) R. C. Murphy & Harper, 1916.

geronticus Gr. old or ageing; *geron, gerontos (γέρων, γέροντος)* old, oldman (43).

giganteus Gr. gigantic; *gigas, gigantos (γίγας, γίγαντος)* giant; mythological human tribe, destroyed by the Gods (macronectes, southern giant-petrel, 30, 654) J. F. Gmelin, 1789.

glacialoides L. icy or frozen, resembling ice; *glaciare* freeze, turn to crystal; Gr. *-oides* resembling (fulmarus, southern fulmar, 32, 656) A. Smith, 1840.

glandarius L. of acorns; *glans,-andis* acorn, nut, bullet (clamator, great spotted cuckoo, 214, 202) C. Linnaeus, 1758.

glareola L. little gravel; *glarea* gravel, thick sand (tringa, wood sandpiper, 166, 357) C. Linnaeus, 1758.

glaucidium Gr. little owl, owlet; diminutive of *glaux, glaukos (γλαῦξ, γλαυκός)* owl; *glaukos (γλαυκός)* which at first meant shining or radiating, and the owl was named due to 'the ferocity of its radiating eyes'; later it came to mean different shades of blue; *glafso (γλαύσσω)* to shine; Eng. glaucoma (33).

glaucurus Gr. blue-grey tailed; *glaucos (γλαυκός)* blue-grey; *oura (οὐρά)* tail (eurystomus, broad-billed roller, 242, 172) P. L. Statius- Müller, 1776.

goliath after the Philistine giant, Goliath of Gath, who was killed by David's slingshot (1 Samuel chapter 17); Hebrew גָּלְיָת (ardea, goliath heron, 62, 590) P. J. Cretzchmar, 1827-1829.

gorsachius from the Japanese name of the black-crowned night-heron *goi-sagi* (*goi* fifth rank; *sagi* heron) ゴイサギ; Jobling (2010, pp. 175) reports the related story; Emperor Daigo (reigned 897-930 AD) ordered a vassal to capture a Black-crowned night heron; the bird surrendered himself and in so doing confirmed the Emperor's omnipotence over nature and man and pleased the Emperor who named it king of herons and gave it the position of fifth rank in his court and set it free (42).

goughensis after Gough Island, where the bird is endemic; it was named after Charles <u>Gough</u> of the Richmond who reported the island in 1732; the island was known as Gonçalo Alvares, after Vasco da Gama's flagship captain, for three centuries and sometimes erroneously as Diego Alvares until Gough sighted it (rowettia, gough finch or gough bunting, 414,) W. E. Clarke, 1904.

gracilirostris L. slender-billed; *gracilis* slender, slight, meagre, poor; *rostrum* bill (acrocephalus, lesser swamp-warbler, 318, 802) G. Hartlaub, 1864.

grallaria L. stilt-walker; *grallae* stilts; *grallator* stilt walker; referring to the bird's long legs (fregetta, white-bellied storm-petrel, 46, 637) L. J. P. Vieillot, 1817.

granatina L. garnet; *granatum* garnet, of dark red colour; *granum* seed, grain; refers to the violet-purple cheeks and ear coverts; garnets are a group of silicate minerals used as gemstones also known as a poor man's rubies; *pomum granatum* (pomegranate) is a fruit that its seeds look like garnets and thus the name (granatina, violet-eared waxbill, 396, 1053) C. Linnaeus, 1766.

granti after William Robert Ogilvie <u>Grant</u> (1863-1924), a Scottish ornithologist and ichthyologist; he was curator of birds at Fettes College, Edinburgh and made a number of collecting trips to Socotra, Madeira and Canary islands; he was also editor of the Bulletin of the British Ornithologists' Club (ptilopsis, southern white-faced scops-owl, 220, 254) P. Kollibay, 1910.

gravis L. heavy; *gravis* heavy, loaded, weighty, grave, serious, important, unpleasant (puffinus, great shearwater, 42, 671) O'Reilly, 1818.

grayi after John Edward *Gray* (1800-1875), a British ornithologist and entomologist; he published a number of works and worked at the British Museum for 50 years as Curator of Birds and head of the Department of Zoology (ammomanopsis, gray's lark, 272, 877) J. A. Wahlberg, 1855.

gregalis L. sociable; *grex, gregis* flock, herd, crowd, company, crew (eremomela, karoo eremomela, 324, 788) A. Smith, 1829.

grillii after Johan Wilhelm *Grill* (1815-1864) Swedish zoologist (Jobling, 2010, pp. 178) (centropus, black coucal, 218, 216) G. Hartlaub, 1861.

griseiventris L. grey-bellied; *griseus* grey; *venter, ventris* stomach, womb, belly (parus, miombo tit, 290, 741) A. Reichenow, 1882.

griseldis Hartlaub named this bird in 1891 but never explained after whom or what; medieval word *griseus*, meaning grey, has been proposed but the name of *Griselda* is a better guess; maybe Boccaccio's? (acrocephalus, Basra reed-warbler, 320, 801); Basra is the name of the port and Governorate at the south of Iraq, where the bird is an almost endemic breeder (breeds in Israel too).

griseocephalus L. & Gr. grey-headed. L. *griseus* grey; Gr. *kephale* (κεφαλή) head (dendropicos, olive woodpecker, 256, 137) P. Boddaert, 1783.

griseopyga L. & Gr. grey-rumped; L. *griseus* grey; Gr. *puge* (πυγή) rump, backside (pseudhirundo, grey-rumped swallow, 280, 747) C. J. Sundevall, 1850.

griseus L. grey; *griseus* grey (passer, northern grey-headed sparrow, 380, 1087, L. J. P. Vieillot, 1817) (puffinus, sooty shearwater, 40, 673, J. F. Gmelin, 1789).

gularis L. of the throat; *gula* throat, neck, gullet, maw, gluttony (crithagra, streaky-headed seedeater, 408, 1129,

A. Smith, 1836) (cuculus, african cuckoo, 212, 208, J. F. Stephens, 1815) (egretta, western reef heron, 64, 586, L. A. G. Bosc, 1792) (nicator, eastern gularis, 296, 776, G. Hartlaub & O. Finsch, 1870).

guinea after Guinea, a country in West Africa; the name derives from Portuguese *Guiné* and refers to the *Guineus,* the black peoples below the Senegal river; *Azenegues* is the Portuguese name for the people north of the river (columba, speckled pigeon, 200, 277) C. Linnaeus, 1758.

gunningi after Dr Jan Willem Bowdewyn <u>Gunning</u> (1860-1913), a Dutch physician who emigrated to South Africa in 1884; he was director of the Staatsmuseum, now the Transvaal museum, founder of the Pretoria National Zoo and co-founder of the African Ornithologists' Union; he also compiled a Checklist of the Birds of South Africa with Alwin Karl Haagner in 1910 (sheppardia, east coast akalat, 312, 926) A. K. Haagner, 1909.

gurneyi after John Henry <u>Gurney</u> (1819-1890), an English banker in Norwich and MP

who was also an amateur ornithologist and worked at the British Natural History Museum; he wrote on birds of England, especially raptors, but also on birds of Africa (zoothera, orange ground-thrush, 298, 901, G. Hartlaub, 1864) (promerops, gurney's sugarbird, 372, 1001, J. P. Verreaux, 1871)

guttata L. speckled, spotted; *gutta* drop, spot, speck, animal and rock spots (zoothera, spotted ground-thrush, 298, 902) N. A. Vigors, 1831.

guttera L. speckled, spotted; *gutta* drop, spot, speck (26).

gutturalis L. of the throat, of the palate; *guttur, gutturis* throat, neck, gullet (irania, irania (white-throated robin), 306, F. E. Guérin-Meneville, 1843) (pterocles, yellow-throated sandgrouse, 198, 339, A. Smith, 1836).

gymnogenys Gr. bare-cheeked; *gymnos (γυμνός)* naked, bare, unarmed; Gr. *genys, genyos (γένυς, γένυος)* cheek, jaw; Eng. <u>gymn</u>astics, <u>gymn</u>asium (turdoides, bare-cheeked babbler, 292, 814) G. Hartlaub, 1865.

gypaetus Gr. vulture eagle; *gyps, gypos (γύψ, γυπός)*

vulture; *aetos (ἀετός)* eagle; *hypaetos (ὑπαετός)* an eagle that looks like a vulture, namely the lamergeier (gypaetus barbatus) (39).

gypohierax Gr. vulture-hawk; *gyps, gypos (γύψ, γυπός)* vulture; *hierax, hierakos (ἱέραξ, ἱέρακος;* Modern Gr. *γεράκι)* hawk, falcon; *iemai (ἵεμαι)* attack, throw oneself at someone (39).

gyps Gr. vulture; *gyps, gypos (γύψ, γυπός)* vulture (40).

H

haemastica Gr. Bloody; refers to the colour of breeding plumage; *haema (αἷμα)* blood; Eng. *haema*toma, *haema*tology, *haema*tite; the common name of the bird is from Hudson Bay, Canada, which was named after Sir Henry *Hudson,* who explored the bay with the Explorer, starting in 1610 (limosa, hudsonian godwit, 170, 347) C. Linnaeus, 1758.

haematopus Gr. blood-footed; *haema (αἷμα)* blood; *pus (ποῦς, ποδός)* foot; *'presumably referring to reddish legs'* (Roberts, 2009) (37).

hagedash both the scientific and popular names of the bird are onomatopoeic renditions of its call (Afrikaans) (bostrychia, hadeda ibis, 76, 609) J. Latham, 1790.

halcyon Gr. kingfisher; *Alcyone (Ἀλκυόνη);* in Gr. mythology, Alcyone was the daughter of Aeolus, god of winds; she was turned into a bird by Zeus and allegedly nests at sea in Gr. winter and for the fourteen days of nesting her father keeps the sea calm; those days are called *halcyon days* or *halcyonids* (30).

haliaetus Gr. sea eagle; *haliaetos (ἁλιαετός)* sea-eagle; *haliaietos (ἁλιαίετος)* in poetry; *als (ἅλς, ἁλός)* salt, sea; *aetos (ἀετός)* eagle (pandion, osprey, 90, 473) C. Linnaeus, 1758.

haliaeetus Gr. sea eagle; *als (ἅλς, ἁλός)* salt, sea; *aetos (ἀετός)* eagle (39).

halli after Robert *Hall* (1867-1949), an Australian naturalist and ornithologist; he was founder, president and curator of many unions, institutions and museums; his collections are in the Tasmanian museum and the Australian National museum in Melbourne, and his Siberian collection is at the Natural History museum at Tring, England (Beolens & Watkins, 2003) (macronectes, northern giant-petrel, 30, 655) G. M. Mathews, 1912.

halobaena Gr. sea-walker, tread at sea; *als (ἅλς, ἁλός)* salt, sea; *baino (μπαίνω)* enter, walk in (46).

hartlaubii after Karel Johan Gustav *Hartlaub* (1814-1900), a German academic and explorer; he was professor of zoology at Bremen and founder of the *Journal für Ornithologie* with Cabanis; he wrote the first descriptions of over thirty southern African birds (Beolens & Watkins, 2003) (chroicocephalus (larus) hartlaub's gull, 184, 444, C. F. Bruch, 1853) (pternistis, hartlaub's spurfowl, 128, 68, J. V. Barbosa du Bocage, 1869) (turdoides, hartlaub's babbler, 292, 810, J. V. Barbosa du Bocage, 1868).

hedydipna Gr. sweet-eating; *hedydeipnos (ἡδύδειπνος)* dinning sweetly or money spending; *hedys (ἡδύς)* sweet, pleasant tasting; *deipno (δεῖπνο)* dinner; in Homer it was the main meal of the day, no matter which time of the day (56).

heliolais Gr. sun warbler; *helios (ἥλιος)* sun; *lais* Jobling writes it is L. for warbler; Gr. *lais (λαϊς)* Doric form of *leeis (ληΐς)* plunder, loot, booty, prey (52).

herero after Herero, a pastoralist, Bantu people of Namibia and Botswana (namibornis, herero chat, 306, 943) M. de Schauensee 1931.

heteromirafra Gr. different (other) mirafra; *heteros (ἔτερος)* different; *mirafra* meaning unknown; it has been suggested *mirus* wonderful, strange, remarkable, amazing; *afer* african but at least one species does not appear in Africa (53).

heuglini after Martin Theodor von *Heuglin* (1824-1876), a German ornithologist; he travelled in Africa and elsewhere and published *Ornithologie Nordost Afrika* (1869), an account of the birds of East Africa; he opposed evolutionary theories, probably because of his father being a protestant pastor; he died of pneumonia (cossypha, white-browed robin-chat, 310, 931) G. Hartlaub, 1866.

hiaticula L. cleft dweller; *hiatus* opening, cleft, crevice, greedy desire, emphasis; *colere* live in, inhabit, dwell and also, adorn, honour, worship (Roberts says the name refers to its habit to breed among pebbles and rocks) Eng. *cult, cul*ture, *cul*tivate(charadrius, common ringed plover, 152, 396) C. Linnaeus, 1758.

himantopus Gr. Roberts agrees with Jobling that *himantopous (ἱμαντόπους)* means *strap-foot* from *himas, himantos (ἱμάς, ἱμάντος)* strap or thong and *pous (ποῦς, ποδός)* foot; the etymology is correct and comes from Pliny but it also means *he who has twisted knees* or *bandy-legged* and looking at this bird's knees this second explanation makes more sense; the L. equivalent would be loripes; it was also the name of a people in Ethiopia (himantopus, black-winged stilt, 150, 391) C. Linnaeus, 1758.

hippolais Gr. a small warbler-like bird mentioned by Aristotle, probably the northern wheatear *oenanthe* oenanthe; in Gr. the name was *hypolais (ὑπολαΐς)* and Linnaeus wrote *hippolais* by mistake (*hippo (ἵππος)* meaning horse in Gr.) *hypo (ὑπό)* means under, beneath, sub; *lais* Jobling writes it is L. for warbler; Gr. *lais (λαΐς)* Doric form of *leeis (ληΐς)*

plunder, loot, booty, prey *Lais* is the name of two ancient courtesans, of Corinth (around 425 BCE) and of Hyccara (died 340 BCE).

hirundo L. swallow; *hirundo* swallow, martin, small bird; referring to swallow-like long wings, forked tail, short legs and graceful flight (Roberts, 2009) (sterna, common tern, 192, 459) C. Linnaeus, 1758.

hirundo L. swallow; *hirundo* swallow, martin, small bird (49).

hirundineus L. of swallows, swallow-like; *hirundo* swallow, martin, small bird. (merops, swallow-tailed bee-eater, 240, 188) A. A. H. Lichtenstein, 1793.

hoeschi after Walter *Hoesch* (1896-1961), a German collector in Namibia between 1930 to his death (anthus, mountain pipit, 350, 1105) E. Stresemann, 1938.

holomelas Gr. all-black, black all-over; *holos (ὅλος)* all, entire, whole; *melas, melanos (μέλας, μέλανος)* black, dark; Eng. *holo*caust, *mela*nine, *mela*noma etc. (psalidoprocne, black saw-wing, 280, 764) C. J. Sundevall, 1850 or E. Rüppel, 1840.

hordeaceus L. of barley; *hordeum* barley (euplectes, black-winged bishop, 388, 1027) C. Linnaeus, 1758.

horus after *Horus*, a deity of ancient Egyptian religion and one of the oldest; the name was *hre* and was pronounced as *haru*, meaning falcon and later became *hor*; Greeks called him *Horos* (Ὧρος); Horus was the son of Osiris and Isis and he was the god of sun, sky and kingship; he was depicted as a falcon or as a man with a falcon head; the falcon is either a lanner falcon or a peregrine falcon; he is the logo of Egyptair and can be seen on the company's planes (apus, horus swift, 230, 242) T. von Heuglin, 1869.

hottentota/hottentottus hottentot is the former name for the indigenous Khoi Khoi (means 'real people' in Khoikhoi) people of southern Africa; Dutch settlers named them Hottentots, immitating the sound of their language; today the term is considered derogatory (anas, hottentot teal, 84, 114, J. F. Gmelin, 1789) (turnix, hottentot buttonquail, 132, 121, C. J. Temminck, 1815).

humeralis L. of the shoulders; *umerus* or *humerus* upper arm, shoulder; this bird has white wing coverts (cossypha, white-throated robin-chat, 310, 930) A. Smith, 1836.

hybrida L. hybrid; at the time of description Pallas thought it to be a hybrid between Black and Common terns; hybrid is the offspring of different parents (animal or plants) and also the child of a Roman and a foreign mother or a free man and a slave; in this sense the word is connected to Gr. *hubris* (ὕβρις) offensive behaviour; in theatre it was usually against the gods and it was punishable; in modern Gr. it means insult (chlidonias, whiskered tern, 196, 468) P. S. Pallas, 1811.

hydrobates Gr. water-walker; *hydor, hydatos* (ὕδωρ, ὕδατος) water; *-bates* (-βάτης) walker from the verb *baino* (βαίνω) to walk; Eng. *hydro-* (45).

hyliota Gr. living in woodland; *hyliotes* (ὑλειώτης) living in woodland; *hyle* (ὕλη) wood, forest, woodland (51).

hypargos Gr. like Argos below; *hypo* (ὑπό) under *Argos* (Ἄργος) or *Argus panoptes* (πανόπτης all-seeing) was the one hundred eyed guardian of the white heifer Io, following Hera's orders; Argos's eyes look like spots and these birds have white spots on flanks (58).

hypoleucus Gr. white underneath; *hypo (ὑπό)* under, beneath or sub; leukos *(λευκός)* white; *hypoleucos (ὑπόλευκος)* pale white; Jobling(2010) says it is a lapsus for *hyperleucos (ὑπερλευκός)* exceedingly white (pp. 199) (actitis, common sandpiper, 166, 360) C. Linnaeus, 1758.

hypoxantha Gr. golden yellow beneath; *hypo (ὑπό)* under, beneath, sub, a little; *xanthos (ξανθός)* gold, yellow, blonde; *hypoxanthos (ὑπόξανθος)* a little yellow (prinia, dragensberg prinia, 338, 846) R. B. Sharpe, 1877.

I

ibis Gr. ibis, a wading bird; *eevis, eevidos (ἶβις, ἴβιδος)* Egyptian bird, eats worms and water animals and divine honours attributed to it (by humans), says Herodot and mentions two different species; originally Greeks called the sacred ibis that; Egyptian *hb, hib* (bubulcus,

cattle egret, 64, 592) C. Linnaeus, 1758 (mycteria, yellow-billed stork, 70, 617) C. Linnaeus, 1766.

icterina Gr. yellow; *ikteros (ἴκτερος)* is jaundice and also a yellow-green bird that Greeks believed that a patient who saw it, was cured from jaundice and the bird would die; they believed the same for a bird they called charadrios *(χαραδριός)*; the prefix ik- in ancient Gr. is associated with the colour yellow; iktis *(ἴκτις)* badger and iktinos *(ἰκτῖνος)* a bird of prey, a hawk, a falcon (hippolais, icterina warbler, 314, 804) L. J. P. Vieillot, 1817.

icteropygialis Gr. yellow-rumped; *ikteros (ἴκτερος)* is jaundice; pyge *(πυγή)* rump, backside, tail (eremomela, yellow-bellied eremomela, 324, 786) F. de Lafresnaye, 1839.

idae after *Ida* Laura Pfeiffer (1797-1858), an Austrian traveller and author, a member of Berlin and Paris geographical societies but not of Royal Geographical Society because she was a woman! Her travels around the world included Madagascar (ardeola, malagasy pond-heron, 66, 595) G. Hartlaub, 1860.

imberbis L. beardless; *barba* beard; *in* + *barba;* Sclater reports that the name 'refers to the entire absence of rictal bristles' (Jobling, 2010, 203); could also mean young or small (anomalospiza, cuckoo finch, 394, 1081) J. Cabanis, 1868.

immutabilis L. unalterable, unchangeable; *in* + *mutabilis; mutabilis* changeable, unstable; *mutare* move, shift, alter; name refers to the fact that juvenile has no distinctive plumage; common name refers to one of its breeding colonies, Laysan island of Northwestern Hawaii (phoebastria, laysan albatross, 26, 645) L. W. Rothschild, 1893.

impetuani *from Zulu name for finch or waxbill Im'tiyane or the Tswana name of a waterhole in W. Griqualand, Cape Province, South Africa* (Jobling, 2010, pp. 203); L. *impetus* attack, rapid motion (?) (emberiza, lark-like bunting, 412, 1133) A. Smith, 1836.

importunus L. troublesome or insolent; referring to loud persistent song that lets other creatures know of human presence; originally *in* + *portus* without entrance, having no harbour; *importunus* inconvenient, annoying, rude,

monstrous, ruthless, cruel, hard (andropadus, sombre greenbul, 296, 770) L. J. P. Vieillot, 1818

incerta L. uncertain, variable; *in* + *certus; incertus* uncertain, unsure, variable, doubtful; *certus* fixed, certain, loyal, constant; Roberts says the name refers to its 'uncertain taxonomic affinity' (pterodroma, atlantic petrel, 36, 660) H. Schlegel, 1863.

indicator L. guide; *indicare* show, reveal, point out, accuse; *Legend has it that the greater honeyguide leads men or the honey badger (melivora capensis) to beehives. Africans leave some honey for the bird or next time the bird will lead them to a leopard or venomous snake* (Jobling, 2010, pp. 204) (indicator, greater honeyguide, 250, 123) A. E. Sparrman, 1777.

indicus from India; the word India derives from the Old Persian word *Hindus* and Sanskrit *Sindhu*, the name for the river Indus (urocolius, red-faced mousebird, 232, 199) J. Latham, 1790.

infuscatus L. dusky; *infuscare* to darken, to corrupt (bradornis, chat flycatcher, 342, 912) A. Smith, 1839.

intermedia/intermedius L. intermediate; in the case of the egret it is smaller than the Great egret and bigger than the Little egret (egretta, yellow-billed egret, 64, 584, J. G. Wagler, 1829) (ploceus, lesser masked-weaver, 384, 1010, E. Rüppell, 1845).

interpres L. messenger, interpreter. *In 1741, Linnaeus visited Gotland and thought Tolk was the name for the ruddy turnstone. In Swedish it means translator or interpeter. However the local word Tolk stalk (legs) refers to the common redshank (tringa totanus)* (Jobling, 2010, pp. 206)(arenaria, ruddy turnstone, 172, 361) C. Linnaeus, 1758.

irania from Iran; Iran derives from Old Iranian word *Aryana*, which means 'Land of the Aryans;' Persia is the name that Ancient Greeks used for the same country; only one record of the bird (gutturalis) in the area, near Williston (Sasol, pp.306) Sinclair & Ryan, 2009.

isabellina L. fawn, greyish-yellow or pale buff. Jobling (2010, pp 207) favours the following story for the name of the colour originating from Queen Isabella I of Castile and Spain (reigned 1474-1504), said to have promised not to change her undergarments until Spain was freed from the Moors, over the Archduchess Isabella who vowed to do the same until Ostend was taken! (oenanthe, isabelline wheatear, 304, 951) C. J. Temminck, 1829.

ispidina Roberts and Jobling agree that the name means 'resembling a kingfisher' or that 'hispida' means kingfisher; *hispida* means hairy, shaggy, rough and desolate in L. (30)

ixobrychus Gr. ixos and bellow; *ixos (ἰξός)* a parasitic plant usually in oak trees, called *viscum* in L. or *ixias (ἰξίας)* a plant called chameleon because its leaves change colour; *brychomai (βρυχῶμαι)* to bellow; refers to habitat and grunting call (42).

J

jacobinus after Jacobins, that is what the Dominican friars are called in Paris, because their convent was attached to the now destroyed church of Saint-Jacques; the pied plumage resembles the traditional black cloak the friars wear over their white habits (clamator, jacobin cuckoo, 214, 200) P. Boddaert, 1783.

jardineii after Sir William *Jardine*, 7th Baronet of Applegarth (1800-1874), who was a Scottish ornithologist who produced the Naturalist's Library from 1833 to 1845; his private museum was said to be the finest of his day (Beolens & Watkins, 2003, pp. 180) (turdoides, arrow-marked babbler, 292, 812) A. Smith, 1836.

juncidis L. of rushes; *juncus,-i* rush; *junceus* made of rushes; *juncosus* full of rushes; Its common name refers to its zit-zit-zit song, given in flight (cisticola, zitting cisticola, 330, 838) C. S. Rafinesque, 1810.

jynx Gr. a tail shaking bird; *iynx, iyggos (ἴυγξ, ἴυγγος)* the name of jynx torquilla that derives from its voice and the Gr. verb *iyzo (ἰύζω)* to scream, to shout; the verb can be found in both the Iliad and the Odyssey; later it meant to scream expressing sorrow; the common name in Gr. refers to the shaking of the tail *seisopygis (σεισοπυγίς)* rump shaker; the Eng. name *wryneck* refers to the shaking of the neck; ancient Gr. wizards and witches used to tie

this bird to a wheel and spinned it aiming at charming the hearts of men and make them obey, so it was used in order to bring back unfaithful lovers (28).

K

kaupifalco after Johann Jakob *Kaup* (1803-1873), a German naturalist, zoologist and author, who believed in an innate mathematical order in nature and he attempted biological classifications based on the Quinarian system; *falco* falcon; probably from *falx, falcis* sickle, scythe, curved blade, pruning knife; (40).

kilimensis after Kilimanjaro, the highest mountain in Africa and the highest free-standing mountain in the world at 5,895 metres; it is a dormant volcanic mountain with three cones; the name is disputed whether it is from kiswahili or wachagga and wether it means 'mountain of greatness' or 'who defeats', among other explanations (nectarinia, bronzy sunbird, 372, 984) G. E. Shelley, 1885.

klaas after Levaiilant's Khoi Khoi (Hottentot) servant, who presumably found the bird in 1784 (Beolens & Watkins, 2003, pp.190) Jobling (2009, 214) reports he was a hunter and collector, who accompanied the French explorer on his expeditions in South Africa (chrysococcyx, klaas's cuckoo, 216, 211) J. F. Stephens, 1815.

kori from Tswana name for the bird, Kgori or Kxhori; the male of the species may well be the heaviest flying bird in the world (ardeotis, kori bustard, 144, 295) W. J. Burchell, 1822.

krameri after Wilhelm Heinrich *Kramer*, an Austrian (or German?) zoologist and author. In 1756 he was among the first to adopt Carl von Linnè's binomial nomenclature (psittacula, rose-ringed parakeet, 208, 229) G. A. Scopoli, 1769.

L

lacteus L. milky, milky white; *lac, lactis* milk (bubo, Verreaux's eagle-owl, 222, 258) C. J. Temminck, 1820.

lagonosticta Gr. spotted flanks; *lagon, lagonos (λαγών, λαγόνος)* flank; *stiktos (στικτός)* spotted; *stizo (στίζω)* cause spots (58).

lais Gr. warbler; *lais (λαϊς)* Doric version of *leis (λῃίς)* plunder, loot, boot; *leizomai (λῃίζομαι)* to rob, to plunder, to loot, to sack; Lais of Hyccara (4th century BC), a very expensive Greek courtesan in Sicily, who followed Hippostratus to Thessaly where local women stoned her to death in the temple of Aphroditi, probably out of jealousy (cisticola, wailing cisticola, 332, 830) G. Hartlaub & O. Finsch, 1870.

lamelligerus L. carry a thin plate; *lamella* thin plate; diminutive of *lamina;* -ger from *gerare* or *gerere* to carry, to bear, to wear; Roberts says it refers to *flattened feathered shafts, especially on underparts* (anastomus, openbill stork, 72, 618) C. J. Temminck, 1823.

lamprotornis Gr. bright or shining bird; *lampros (λαμπρός)* bright, brilliant, radiant; *lamprotes (λαμπρότης)* splendour, brightness; *ornis (ὄρνις)* bird in ancient Gr.; the word for bird was both male and female in ancient Gr. In modern Gr. it is only female and it means chicken (55).

laniarius L. like lanius (like a butcher); *laniarius, -ari* connected to pulling to pieces; *lanius, lanii* butcher; *laniare* tear, mangle, mutilate, pull to pieces (48).

lanioturdus L. shrike-like thrush, butcher thrush; *lanius, lanii* butcher; *laniare* tear, mangle, mutilate, pull to pieces; *turdus* thrush (48).

lanius L. butcher; *lanius, lanii* butcher; *laniare* tear, mangle, mutilate, pull to pieces; shrikes were called butchers because they store their prey by impaling it on thorns and sharp twigs, which looks like a butcher's slaughterhouse (Jobling, 2010, pp. 219) (48).

lapponica after Lapponia or Lapland; an area inhabited by the Sami people or Lapps; it stretches over Norway, Sweden, Finnland and Russia (limosa, bar-tailed godwit, 170, 347) C. Linnaeus, 1758.

larus Gr. gull; *laros* (λάρος) rapacious seabird, gull (38).

larvata/larvatus L. masked or bewitched; *larva* evil spirit, demon, horrific mask, ghost; *larvare* bewitch, enchant (aplopelia, lemon dove, 200, 280, C. J. Temminck, 1809) (oriolus,

black-headed oriole, 286, 682, M. Lichtenstein, 1823).

layardi after Edgar Leopold *Layard* (1824-1900), a British diplomat and naturalist; he was a curator of the South African Museum and published *The Birds of South Africa* in 1867, describing 702 species (it was later updated by Sharpe); he worked in Ceylon (Sri Lanka), Cape Colony (South Africa), Brazil, Fiji and New Caledonia (parisoma, layard's tit-babbler, 328, 815) G. Hartlaub, 1862.

leadbeateri after Benjamin *Leadbeater* (1760-1837) a taxidermist, merchant of natural objects in London and ornithologist (bucorvus, southern ground-hornbill, 244, 158) N. A. Vigors, 1825.

leptoptilos Gr. slender plumes; *leptos,-ou (λεπτός,-οῦ)* thin, slender, delicate; *ptilon* (πτίλον) feather, plume (44).

lepturus Gr. slender-tailed; *leptos,-ou (λεπτός,-οῦ)* thin, slender, delicate; *oura (οὐρά)* tail (phaethon, white-tailed tropicbird, 50, 565) F. M. Daudin, 1802.

leschenaultii after Jean Baptiste Louis Claude Theodore

Leschenault de la Tour (1773-1826) a French botanist and ornithologist; he didn't write much but his collections were used by other naturalists; he travelled and collected in Australia, Java, Brasil, Guyana, Africa and elsewhere (charadrius, greater sand plover, 154, 405) R. P. Lesson, 1826.

lessonii after René Primavére *Lesson* (1794-1849), a very important and influential French ornithologist, herpetologist and naturalist; he travelled and wrote about birds and other animals and plants; his texts about birds include *Manuel d'Ornithologie, Histoire Naturelle des Oiseaux-Mouches, Histoire Naturelle des Colibris* and many more (pterodroma, white-headed petrel, 36, 659) P. Garnot, 1826.

leucocephala Gr. white-headed; *leukos (λευκός)* white, bright, clear; *kephali (κεφάλι)* head (halcyon, grey-headed kingfisher, 236, 177) P. L. S. Müller, 1776.

leucogaster Gr. White-bellied; *leukos (λευκός)* white, bright, clear; *gaster, gastros (γαστήρ, γαστρός)* belly; the booby's common name comes from the Spanish slang term *bobo*, which means stupid; Eng. *gastric, gastritis, gastronomy* (cinnyricinclus, violet-backed starling, 366, 968, P. Boddaert, 1783) (sula, brown booby, 52, 569, P. Boddaert, 1783).

leucolaema Gr. white-throat; *leukos (λευκός)* white, bright, clear; *laemos (λαιμός)* throat (serinus, damara canary, 410) R. B. Sharpe, 1903.

leucomelas Gr. white and black; *leukos (λευκός)* white, bright, clear; *melas, melanos (μέλας, μέλανος)* black, dark (calonectris, streaked shearwater, 40, 671, C. J. Temminck, 1835) (tockus, southern yellow-billed hornbill, 246, 152, M. Lichtenstein, 1842) (tricholaema, acacia pied barbet, 254, 144, P. Boddaert, 1783).

leuconotus Gr. white-backed; *leukos (λευκός)* white, bright, clear; *noton* or *notos* or *nota (νῶτον* or *νῶτος* or *νῶτα)* the back of humans and vertebrate animals (gorsachius, white-backed night-heron, 66, 598, J. G. Wagler, 1827) (thalassornis, white-backed duck, 80, 87, Eyton, 1838).

leucophrys Gr. white-browed; *leukos (λευκός)* white, bright, clear; *ophrys, ophryos (ὀφρύς,* ὀφρύος) eyebrow; frythi *(φρύδι)* eybrow in modern Gr. (anthus, plain-backed pipit, 352, 1105, L. J. P. Vieillot, 1818) (cercotrichas, white-browed scrub-robin, 308, 939, L. J. P. Vieillot, 1817).

leucoptera/us Gr. white-winged; leukos *(λευκός)* white, bright, clear; *pteron (πτερόν)* wing, feather; *ftero (φτερό)* in modern Gr. (chlidonias, white-winged tern, 196, 469, C. J. Temminck, 1815) (crithagra, protea seed-eater 408, 1128, R. B. Sharpe 1871).

leucorhoa Gr. white-rumped; *leukos (λευκός)* white, bright, clear; *orros (ὄρρος)* the edge of the coccyx, the edge where tail feathers of birds emerge; Jobling (2010, pp. 225) writes it *leucorrhoa* and I believe he is right since the word in Gr. is written with a double r (ρ); its common name refers to William Elford *Leach* (1790-1836), a British zoologist who sent the specimen to Vieillot to describe it; he was employed by the British Museum and became an expert on crustaceans; he wrote the *Zoological miscellany* in 1814 (oceanodroma, Leach's storm-petrel, 44, 639) L. J. P. Vieillot, 1817.

leucotis Gr. white-eared; *leukos (λευκός)* white, bright, clear; *ous,*

otos *(οὖς, ὠτός)* ear; *afti (αυτί)* in modern Gr. (eremopterix, chestnut-backed sparrow-lark, 272, 887, E. Smith-Stanley, 1814) (stactolaema, white-eared barbet, 252, 138, C. J. Sundevall, 1850).

levaillantii after Francois <u>Le Vaillant</u> (1753-1824), a French traveller, explorer, collector, naturalist and ornithologist; born in Dutch Guiana (Surinam) he later travelled around southern Africa; he gave french names to birds, rejecting Linnaeus's systematic nomenclature; most notable of course is the name he gave the 'Bateleur'; his relationship with a Khoikhoi woman whom he named Narina after a flower and then named the trogon after her, was scandalous for colonial Europe (clamator, levaillant's cuckoo, 214, 201, W.J. Swainson, 1829) (scleroptila, 130, 65, A. Vallenciennes, 1825).

levaillantoides Gr. like genus levaillant; *-oides (-οειδές)* resembling (scleroptila, orange river francolin, 130, 67) A. Smith, 1836.

libonyana/us *'Tswana name Lebonyana for the red-billed buffalo weaver bubalornis niger, given erroneously to the* *kurrichane thrush which also has a red bill'* (Jobling, 2009, pp. 226) (turdus, kurrichane thrush, 298, 905) A. Smith, 1836.

lilianae Jobling reports that the bird was named after 'Lilian Sclater (fl.1909) British naturalist and traveller in East Africa'; Lilian Elizabeth Lutley Sclater travelled with her brother, William Lutley Sclater to Nyasaland, now Malawi (agapornis, Lilian's lovebird, 208, 228) G. E. Shelley, 1894

limicola L. mud-dweller; *limus, -i* mud, slime, filth, mire; *colere* live in, inhabit, dwell (36).

limnodromus Gr. lake-racer; *limne (λίμνη)* lake, marsh; *dromos (δρόμος)* road, route, path, course, race, run; *dromeas (δρομέας)* runner, racer (1141).

limosa L. muddy; *limus, -i* mud, slime, filth, mire; refers to non-breeding habitat, according to Roberts (limosa, black-tailed godwit, 170, 346) C. Linnaeus, 1758.

lineiventris L. striped below; *linea* line; *venter, ventris* belly; Eng. *ventri*cle, *ventri*loquism, *ventri*loquist (anthus, striped pipit, 352, 1101) C. J. Sundevall, 1850.

lioptilus Gr. smooth-plumed; *lios (λεῖος)* smooth, glossy; *ptilon (πτίλον)* feather, wing, plume (51).

lissotis Gr. smooth bustard; ancient Gr. *lissos (λισσός)* smooth, plain; *otis (ὠτίς* bustard (34).

litsitsirupa onomatopoeic rendition of call (Tswana according to Jobling, 2009, pp. 228) (psophocichla, groundscraper thrush, 298, 903) A. Smith, 1836.

livia L. bluish or leaden colour; *livere* to be livid or discoloured (columba, rock, dove, 200, 276) J. F. Gmelin, 1789.

livingstonei /livingstonii after David Livingstone (1813-1873), undoubtedly the most famous explorer of Africa; he was a Scottish doctor and missionary, anti-slavery crusader; he was the first Euopean to see the Victoria Falls which he named, or after rev. Charles Livingstone (1821-1873), brother of David Livingstone and his secretary on his Zambezi expedition (1858-1863) (erythrocercus, livingstone's flycatcher, 326, 777, G. R. Gray, 1870) (tauraco, livingstone's tauraco, 210, 245, G. R. Gray, 1864).

lobatus Gr. lobed, in reference to the toes (Roberts, 2009); *lovos* (λοβός) lobe (phalaropus, red-necked phalarope, 174, 378) C. Linnaeus, 1758.

locustella L. small locust; *locusta, -ae* locust, crustacean, lobster; *ell* little, small (paludipasser, locustfinch, 398, 1038) S. A. Neave, 1909.

longicaudatus L. long-tailed; *longus* long, tall; *cauda* tail (anthus, long-tailed pipit, 352, 1108) R. Liversidge, 1996.

longicaudus L. long-tailed; *longus* long, tall; *cauda* tail (stercorarius, long-tailed jaeger, 182, 436) L. J. P. Vieillot, 1819.

longuemarei after Henri Victor Guoye de *Longuemare* (b. 1823) a French amateur collector (anthreptes, western violet-backed sunbird, 374, 975) R.P. Lesson, 1831 or 1833.

lophaetus Gr. crested eagle; *lophos* (λόφος) crest, animal neck; in anc. Gr. it first meant the neck of animals and then the crest of a helmet and hill; in modern Greek it still means hill but not crest which is *lophion* (λοφίον); *aetos* (ἀετός) eagle (40).

lophotis Gr. crested bustard; *lophos* (λόφος) crest, animal neck; in anc. Gr. it first meant the neck of animals and then the crest of a helmet and hill; in modern Greek it still means hill but not crest which is *lophion* (λοφίον); *otis* (ὠτίς) bustard (34).

luapula after *Luapula* river; it forms part of the border between Zambia and the DR Congo; it joins Lake Bangweulu in Zambia to Lake Mweru, which belongs to both countries; it is part of Africa's second longest river, the Congo. (cisticola, luapula cisticola, 334, 832) H. Lynes, 1933.

lucidus L. bright; *lucidus* bright, shining, clear, transparent; *lux, lucis* light, daylight, day, life (phalacrocorax, white-breasted cormorant, 54, 575) M. Lichtenstein, 1823.

ludwigii after Carl Ferdinand Heinrich Freiherr von *Ludwig* (1784-1847), a German pharmacist who sailed to Capetown in 1805 and became a well known collector of natural specimens, which he sent to Europe (dicrurus, square-tailed drongo, 284, 683, A. Smith, 1834) (neotis, ludwig's bustard, 144, 293, E. Rüppell, 1837).

lugensa L. mourning; *lugere* mourn, grieve, lament, bewail, be in mourning (46).

lugubris L. mournful, mourning, grievous, sorrowful; *lugere* mourn, grieve, lament, bewail, be in mourning. (vanellus, senegal lapwing, 156, 413) R. Lesson, 1826.

luscinia L. nightingale; *luscinia* nightingale; *lux+cano* light+sing because nightingales sing at dawn (luscinia, thrush nightingale, 312, 927) C. Linnaeus, 1758.

lybius a bird mentioned by Aristotle and Aristophanes possibly related to woodpeckers (Roberts, 2009, pp. 28); *libyos (λιβυός)* unknown bird; the name *Libue* (Λιβύη) was used by anc. Greeks to denote Northwest Africa (28).

M

maccoa an alternative spelling of Macao or in Portuguese Macau; the maccoa duck can be found only in Africa; Macao is a peninsula and two islands, Taipa and Coloane; it used to be a Portuguese colony and now belongs to China; it is the most densely populated area in the world and one of the richest; *'the Afrikaans names for the domestic Muscovy Duck and the Spur-winged Goose are Makou and Wilde Makou respectively, but that Makou is of Chinese origin* (Clinning, 1989 at Jobling, 2010, pp. 234)(oxyura, maccoa duck, 80, 89) T. C. Eyton, 1838.

maccormicki after Dr Robert McCormick (1800-1890,), a British naval surgeon, polar explorer, and naturalist, who collected the specimen in Antarctica in 1841; he was on the Beagle but left it as he was irritated by Darwin collecting specimens instead of him; he visited Cape Verde twice and took part in Antarctic expeditions; he wrote *Voyages of Discovery in the Arctic and Antarctic Seas, and Round the World: Being Personal Narratives of Attempts to Reach the North and South Poles;* and also an account of an *Open-Boat Expedition up the Wellington Channel in Search of Sir John Franklin and Her Majesty's Ships Erebus and Terror, in Her Majesty's Boat Forlorn Hope, under the Command of the Author* (Beolens & Watkins, 2003, pp.227) (catharacta, south polar skua, 182, 433) H. Saunders, 1893.

macheiramphus Gr. dagger-like bill; *machaira (μάχαιρα)* knife, dagger; *ramphos (ράμφος)* bill, beak (39).

macrodipterix Gr. long double wing; *macros (μακρός)* long, great; *dis (δίς) two, double; pteryx, pterygos (πτέρυξ, πτέρυγος)* wing (33).

macronectes Gr. long or great swimmer; *macros (μακρός)* long, great; *nektes (νήκτης)* swimmer; *nekho (νήχω)* swim (46).

macronyx Gr. long claw; *macros (μακρός)* long, great; *onyx, onychos (ὄνυξ, ὄνυχος)* claw, nail (59).

macroptera Gr. long-winged; *macros (μακρός)* long, great; *pteron (πτερόν)* wing; in modern Gr the p has become f and thus it is *ftero (φτερό)* (pterodroma, great-winged petrel, 36, 659) A. Smith, 1840.

macroura/macrourus Gr. long tailed; *macros (μακρός)* long, great; *oura (οὐρά)* tail (circus, pallid harrier, 106, 503, S. G. Gmelin, 1770) (euplectes, yellow-mantled widowbird, 390,

1032, J. F. Gmelin, 1789) (vidua, pin-tailed whydah, 392, 1070, P. S. Pallas, 1764).

maculosa L. spotted; *macula* spot, stain, taint; *maculare* to stain, defile; *maculosa* spotted, disreputable (prinia, karoo prinia, 338, 845) P. Boddaert, 1783.

madagascariensis from Madagascar; Madagascar is an island country in the Indian Ocean, off the shore of South East Africa; the main island known as Madagascar is the fourth largest island in the world and 90% of its plants and animals can be found nowhere else in the world as a result of the isolation they live in as a result of supercontinent Gondwana's breakup; Madagascar broke up from the Indian peninsula some 88 million years ago (porphyrio, african purple swamphen, 136, 330) J. Latham, 1801.

magellanicus after Portuguese explorer *Ferdinand Magellan* (Por. Fernhao de Magalhaes) (1480-1521) who spotted the birds in 1520; he organised an expedition to the East Indies from 1519 to 1522 which resulted in the first circumnavigation of the Earth; Magellan never completed the voyage as he was killed in the Battle of Mactan in the Philippines in 1521 (spheniscus, magellanic penguin, 16, 634) J. R. Forster, 1781.

magnirostris L. great-billed; *magnus* great; *rostrum, rostris* bill, beak (galerida, large-billed lark, 260, 895) J. F. Stephens, 1826.

mahali Tswana name *Mogale* or *Muxali* bold person (Jobling, 2010, pp 238) (plocepasser, white-browed sparrow-weaver, 382, 1006) A. Smith, 1836.

malaconotus Gr. soft-backed; *malakos (μαλακός)* soft; *noton* or *notos* or *nota (νῶτον* or *νῶτος* or *νῶτα)* the back of humans and vertebrate animals; refers to soft, fluffy back and rump feathers (Roberts, 2009) (48).

malcorus Gr. soft-tailed; *malakos (μαλακός)* soft; *oura* ουρά tail (52).

malimbicus the Limba or *Malimba* people are an ethnic group of Cameroon; *Malimbe* is a type of xylophone from the Congo or a lamellophone or mbira type instrument of the Nyamwezi, the second largest ethnic group of Tanzania

(merops, rosy bee-eater, 240, 1140) G. Shaw, 1806.

mandingoa after *Mandingo* tribe from Niger river valley in west Africa, also known as *Mandinka, Malinke* or *Mandinko;* they belong to the *Mandé* group of people and now live in many countries of West Africa (57).

manoensis after Mano area, west of lake Nyassa (now Malawi) in Zambia (Jobling, 2010, pp. 240); *Mano* is also a river in West Africa and a people of Liberia (cinnyris, miombo double-collared sunbird, 376, 987) A. Reichenow, 1907.

margaritatus Gr. adorned with pearls; *margaritari (μαργαριτάρι)* pearl; L. *margarita* pearl; probably of Persian origin *murwari* (hypargos, pink-throated twinspot, 400, 1058) Strickland, 1844.

marginalis L. marginal, pertaining to the margins or edges; *margo* margin, edge, rim, border; refers to the white edged feathers of the upperparts of the bird (aenigmatolimnas, striped crake, 138, 329) G. Hartlaub, 1857.

marginatus L. bordered or edged; *margo* margin, edge,

rim, border; Roberts writes *'of the edge, in this case the shore'*, 2010) (charadrius, white-fronted plover, 154, 403) L. J. P. Vieillot, 1818.

marina L. marine; *marinus* marine; *mare, maris* sea, sea-water, ocean, the colour blue (pelagodroma, white-faced storm-petrel, 48, 636) J. Latham, 1790.

mariquensis after Marico or Madikwe river in Southern Africa; it starts as the *Groot Marico*, near Rustenburg, South Africa, and after meeting other rivers, such as the Crocodile river, it becomes the Limpopo river (bradornis, marico flycatcher, 342, 914, A. Smith, 1847) (cinnyris, marico sunbird, 376, 998, A. Smith, 1836).

martinicus from *Martinique;* Martinique is an island of the Lesser Antilles in the eastern Carribean Sea and is one of 27 France's overseas regions and thus is a member of the European Union and its currency is the Euro; the name was given to the island by Cristopher Columbus, who sighted the island in 1493 and landed on it in 1502 (porphyrio, american purple gallinule, 136, 333) C. Linnaeus, 1766.

matsudaire after Viscount Yorikatsu *Matsudaira* (1876-1945) who collected the type specimen; he was a Japanese ornithologist who wrote *A Hand-list of the Japanese birds,* in 1922; the petrels only breed off the shore of Japan on a few rocky islets (Beolens & Watkins, 2003, pp. 223) (oceanodroma, Matsudaira's storm-petrel, 44, 640) N. Kuroda, 1922.

mauretanicus of *Mauritania;* Mauritania, the 11th largest country in Africa that is part of the Magreb region in North West Africa; almost 90% of the country lies within the Sahara desert and thus the majority of the three and a half million people live in the south of the country; the name derives from the Berber *Kingdom of Mauretania* which existed in the North west corner of Africa for a thousand years since the 3rd century BC (puffinus, Balearic shearwater, 42, 675) P. R. Lowe, 1921.

maurus Moorish, African, of Mauritania; Gr black; *mauros (μαῦρος)* black, dark (circus, black harrier, 106, 502) C. J. Temminck, 1828.

maxima/maximus L. greatest; *maximus* greatest, biggest, largest, longest; superlative of *magnus* great, big, large, long (megaceryle, giant kingfisher, 234, 183, P. S. Pallas, 1769) (sterna, royal tern, 190, 452, P. Boddaert, 1783).

media L. intermediate; *media* half, middle, common neutral; in size between Common snipe (*gallinago gallinago*) and Eurasian Woodcock (*scolopax rusticola*)(gallinago, great snipe, 172, 342) J. Latham, 1787.

megaceryle Gr. great kingfisher; *megas (μέγας)* great, large, big; *ceryle (κηρύλος)* kingfisher; the type *keirylos (κειρύλος)* was constructed by Aristophanes and thus named Sporgilos the barber from the verb *keiro (κείρω)* to cut hair and would loosely translate as razor bird (30).

melaenornis Gr. black bird; *melas (μέλας)* black; *ornis (ὄρνις)* bird in ancient Gr.; the word for bird was both male and female in ancient Gr.; in modern Gr. it is female and it means chicken (54).

melanocephala Gr. black-headed; *melas (μέλας)* black; *kephale (κεφαλή)* head in Ancient Gr. and *(κεφάλι)* in modern Gr (apalis, black-headed apalis, 326, 854, G. Fischer & A. Reichenow, 1884)(ardea, black-headed heron, 62, 589, J. G. Children & N. A. Vigors 1826).

melanogaster Gr. black-bellied; *melas (μέλας)* black; *gaster, gasteros (γαστήρ, γαστέρος)* belly; Eng. *gastric, gastr*itis, *gastro*nomy (lissotis, black-bellied bustard, 146, 306) E. Rüppel, 1835.

melanogenis Gr. black-cheeked; *melas (μέλας)* black; *genys, genyos (γένυς, γένυος)* cheek, jaw; its common name refers to the Crozet islands, named after Jules *Crozet,* second in command of the French expedition, led by Marc-Joseph Marion du Fresne, that discovered this sub-antarctic archipelago in 1772 (phalacrocorax, crozet shag, 54, PP King, 1828).

melanoleuca/melanoleucus Gr. black and white; *melas (μέλας)* black; *leucos (λευκός)* white; of the two subspecies of sparrowhawks only A. m. melanoleucus occurs in the region (accipiter, black sparrowhawk, 108, 520, Dr Sir A. Smith, 1830) (corvinella, magpie shrike, 358, 729, W. Jardine,

1831) (tringa, greater yellowlegs, 168, 355, J. F. Gmelin, 1798).

melanophrys Gr. black-browed; *melas (μέλας)* black; *ophrys, ophryos (ὀφρύς, ὀφρύος)* eyebrow; frythi (φρύδι) eybrow in modern Gr. (thalassarche, black-browed albatross, 26, 649) C. J. Temminck, 1828.

melanops Gr. black-faced; *melas (μέλας)* black; *ops, opos (ὤψ, ὠπός)* eye, face; cycl*ops* means circular eye (turdoides, black-faced babbler, 292, 810) G. Hartlaub, 1867.

melanopterus Gr. black-winged; *melas (μέλας)* black; *pteron (πτερόν)* wing (vanellus, black-winged lapwing, 156, 415) P. J. Cretzchmar, 1829.

melanotis Gr. black eared; *melas μέλας* black; *ous, otos (οὖς, ὠτός)* ear (anaplectes, red-headed weaver, 384, 1022, F. de Lafresnaye, 1839) (coccopygia, swee waxbil, 402, 1044, C. J. Temminck, 1823)

melanotos Gr. black backed; *melas μέλας* black; *noton* or *notos* or *nota (νῶτον* or *νῶτος* or *νῶτα)* the back of humans and vertebrate animals (calidris, pectoral sandpiper, 160, 371, L.

J. P. Vieillot, 1819) (sarkidiornis, comb duck, 78, 98, T. Pennant, 1769).

melanurus Gr. black-tailed; *melas (μέλας)* black; *oura (οὐρά)* tail (passer, cape sparrow, 380, 1085) P. L. Statius Müller, 1776.

melba Jobling (2010, pp. 248) reports that Linnaeus left no explanation for this name; a suggestion that it could be short for *melas* and *alba (melas μέλας* black in Gr. *alba* white in L.) *melalba* and *melba* certainly would make sense but Linnaeus was not as playful with words! (pytilia, green-winged pytilia, 398, 1058, C. Linnaeus, 1758) (tachymarptis, alpine swift, 228, 234, C. Linnaeus, 1758).

meleagris Meleager was a hero in Gr. mythology, who hunted and killed the Calydonian boar with the help of Atalanta; his mother, Althaea, put a brand of wood in the fire and this led to his death as predicted by the Fates; Althea did this when Meleager killed her son and her brother; the women who mourned Meleager's death (his sisters or daughters) were turned into guineafowl (Meleagrides) (numida, helmeted guineafowl, 124, 82) C. Linnaeus, 1758.

melierax Gr. melodious hawk; *melos (μέλος)* song, choral or lyric song; *hierax hierakos (ἱέραξ, ἱέρακος)* falcon, hawk; maybe from *ieros (ἱερός)* sacred, holy since the hawk was the sacred bird of Apollo (Aristophanes, Birds, 516); Eng. *melo*dy (40).

meliphilus Gr. honey-loving; *meli (μέλι)* honey; *philos (φίλος)* friend, loving; *phileo (φιλέω)* love; Eng. *philo*sophy, *philo*logy (indicator, pallid honeyguide, 250, 126) H. C. Oberholzer, 1905.

melocichla Gr. melodious thrush; *melos (μέλος)* song, choral or lyric song; *kikhle* or *cichla (κίχλη* or *τσίχλα)* thrush (51).

menelli after Frederic Philip *Mennell* (b. 1880), a geologist and curator of the Bulawayo Museum, Southern Rhodesia, now Zimbabwe (crithagra, black-eared seedeater, 408, 1130) C. Chubb, 1908.

mentalis L. chinned, pertaining to the chin; *mentum* chin; in reference to malar stripe says Roberts (2009) (melocichla, moustached grass-warbler, 320, 782) L. Fraser, 1843.

merops Gr. bee-eater; *merops, meropos (μέροψ, μέροπος)*

bee-eater, specifically the European bee-eater *merops apiaster;* it was used in poetry to signify articulated people, 'people who divided voices' (30).

metabates Gr. he who goes from one place to another, leaper, vaulter; *meta (μετά-)* of passing to something new; *vaino (βαίνω)* to walk, to tread; *metavaino (μεταβαίνω)* to go from one place to another; *metabates (μεταβάτης)* he who moves from one place to place (melierax, dark chanting hawk, 112, 508) M. T. von Heuglin, 1861.

mevesii After Friedrich Wilhelm *Meves* (1814-1891), a German zoologist, curator at the Riksmuseet's (the Royal Museum), Stocholm, zoological department (1841-1877), under whom Wahlberg studied; he published *Overview of Royal Science Academy Collections*, in 1854, *Contribution to Swedish Ornithology*, in 1868 and *Ornithological Observations in Northwest Russia 1869*, in 1871, among several other works (lamprotornis, meves's starling, 368, 967) J. A. Wahlberg, 1856.

meyeri after Dr Bernhard *Meyer* (1767-1836), a German physician, botanist, ornithologist and collector; he co authored books about plants and birds; among them were *Naturgeschichte der Vögel Deutschlands* in 1805 and *Taschenbuch der deutschen Vögelkunde (1810-1822)*, both with Johann Wolf (poicephalus, meyer's parrot, 206, 223) P. J. Cretzschmar, 1827.

microparra Gr. small parra; *mikros (μικρός)* small, little; *parra* a bird never really identified; *parra* is Spanish for vine (especially artificially raised) and in Guatemala it is a special vine that produces drinking water for walkers; Eng. *micro* (37).

migrans L. migrant, wanderer; *migrare* to migrate, to move, change residence, pass away, to transport, go away, depart (milvus, black kite, 112, 479) P. Boddaert, 1783.

milanjensis after the Milanji Hills, Nyassaland (Malawi); it is now called the Mulanje Massif or mountain, koppie in Afrikaans and it is found at the south of Malawi, near Blantyre (andropadus, stripe-cheeked greenbul, 296,772) G.E. Shelley, 1894.

milvus L. kite; *milvus, milvi* (or *milvius* or milvuus)kite; in Egyptian mythology Isis is said to have taken the form of a kite many times, to resurrect the dead (39).

minor L. small; *minor* smaller, less, inferior, younger (comparative of *parvus* small); Eng. *minor*ity (chionis, lesser sheathbill, 178, G. Hartlaub, 1841) (eudyptula, little penguin, 16, J. R. Foster, 1781) (fregata, greater frigatebird, 58, 627, J. F. Gmelin, 1789)(indicator, lesser honeyguide, 250, 124, J. F. Stephens, 1815) (lanius, lesser grey shrike, 358, 727, J. F. Gmelin, 1788) (phoenicopterus, lesser flamingo, 74, 606, E. Geoffroy-Saint Hilaire 1798)(pyrenestes, lesser seedcracker, 400, 1052, G. E. Shelley, 1894)

minullus L. very small; *minulus* diminutive of *minus* small, little, unimportant, (accipiter, little sparrowhawk, 110, 516). F.M. Daudin, 1800.

minuta/us L. small; *minutus* small, insignificant, petty, tiny; *minuere* to make smaller, lessen, reduce, diminish (anthoscous, cape pendulin-tit, 324, 736 G. Shaw, 1812) (calidris, little stint, 164, 366, J. P. A. Leisler, 1812) (ixobrychus, little bittern, 68, 599, C. Linnaeus, 1766).

mirafra *mirafra* meaning unknown; it has been suggested *mirus* wonderful, remarkable, amazing, extraordinary and *afer* african but at least one species does not appear in Africa; other suggestions include Javanese or other local names (53).

molitor L. miller; *molitor* miller. Roberts (2009, pp. 716) reports that the name refers to the bird's 'stone rubbing call'; Jobling (2010, pp. 258) suggests that *Molenar* was the name given by Levaillant to Batis *capensis* in 1805, from Cape Dutch word *moolenar* miller, 'from the supposed resemblance of the song of the male to the grinding of mill-stones' (batis, chinspot batis, 346, 716) Küster, 1836.

mollis L. soft; *mollis* soft, gentle, tender, smooth; *mollire* soften, tame, make easier; refers to the bird's soft plumage (pterodroma, soft-plumsged petrel, 36, 661) J. Gould, 1844.

monachus Gr. a monk (hooded); *monachos (μοναχός)* monk; *monos (μόνος)* solitary, single, alone, only (necrosyrtes, hooded vulture, 88, 486) C. J. Temminck, 1823.

mongolus from Mongolia; *Mongolia* is a landlocked country in central Asia, bordered by Russia and China; almost 30% of the population are nomadic or semi nomadic as there is little arable land; most of the country is covered by grassy steppe with mountains to the north and west and the Gobi desert to the south (charadrius, lesser sand-plover, 154, 404) P. S. Pallas, 1776.

monogrammicus Gr. single-lined; *monos (μόνος)* single, only, alone, solitary; *grammikos (γραμμικός)* linear; *gramme (γραμμή)* line; Eng. *gramma*r, *monogram* (kaupifalco, lizard buzzard, 114, 507) C. J. Temminck, 1824.

montanus L. montane, of the mountains; *montanus* mountainous, mountain-, highland; *mons, montis* mountain, huge rock (cercococcyx, barred long-tailed cuckoo, 216, 210) J. P. Chapin, 1928.

monteiri after Joachim Joao *Monteiro* (1833-1878), a Portuguese mining engineer who collected natural history specimens in Angola, from 1860 to 1875; he wrote *Angola and the river Congo* (Beolens &

Watkins, 2003, pp. 239)(tockus, Monteiro's hornbill, 246, 148) G. Hartlaub, 1865.

monticola L. highlander, mountain dweller; *monticola* mountaineer, highlander; *mons, montis* mountain; *cola* inhabitant; *colere* to dwell, inhabit, live in (oenanthe, mountain wheatear, 302, 948) L. J. P Vieillot, 1818.

moquini after Christian Horace Bénédict Alfred *Moquin*-Tandon (1804-1863), a French malacologist (people who study mollusks), ornithologist and collector (haematopus, african black oystercatcher, 150, 389) C. L. Bonaparte, 1856.

morio L. contraction of mormorion a dark brown stone (Roberts, 2009), black quartz (Jobling, 2010, pp. 260); L. *morio* fool, idiot kept as a laughing-stock, jester (onychognathus, red-winged starling, 368, 961) C. Linnaeus, 1766.

morus Gr. silly, foolish, sluggish, lazy; *moros (μωρός)* silly, fool, stupid; refers to reports of how easy it was to approach, capture or kill gannets and boobies in their breeding colonies (41).

moseleyi after Prof. Henry Nottidge *Moseley* (1844-1891), a British zoologist and explorer. He travelled on HMS Challenger around the world between 1872 and 1876, collecting many specimens and wrote an account of the expedition in 1879; he took part in expeditions to Ceylon (Sri Lanka), California and Oregon; he was head of the Department of Zoology and Comparative Anatomy of the Pitt Rivers Museum in Oxford; he has many species and even genera named after him (Beolens & Watkins, 2003, pp. 241) (eudyptes, northern rockhopper penguin, 16) G. Mathews & T. Iredale, 1921.

motacilla L. wagtail; *motare* keep moving; *motus* movement, dance, gesture; -*cilla* Jobling (2010, pp. 261) reports is mistaken for tail since medieval times, 'Varro's name for the wagtail' (59).

motitensis after *Motito* or *Motitong*, a Tswana township near Old Latakoo, 135 miles north of Orange River, South Africa (Jobling, 2010, pp. 261) (passer, great sparrow, 380, 1084) A. Smith, 1836.

mozambica/us of Mozambique; *Moçambique* is a country in southeast Africa; the country was named after the island of Mozambique by the Portuguese; the name derives from *Musa Al Big* or *Mossa Al Bique* or *Mussa Ben Mbiki*, an Arab trader who first visited the island and later lived there (crithagra, yellow-fronted canary, 406, 1118) P. L. Statius-Müller, 1776.

muscicapa L. flycatcher; *musca, -ae* fly, gadfly, bothering person; *capere* to catch, to take, to seize, to capture, to arrest (54).

musicus Gr. musical; *mousike (μουσική)* music, any art form protected by the Muses, especially music and lyric poetry; *Muses (Μοῦσες)* in Gr. mythology the goddesses of art and sciences; Eng. *music, museum* (bias, black and white flycatcher, 342, 711) L. J. P. Vieillot, 1818.

musophaga Arabic & Gr. banana-eater; *musa* botanical genus *musa* plantain, banana; Arabic موز *mauz* banana; Gr. *phagein (φαγεῖν)* to eat (infinitive of *ephagon (ἔφαγον)* (I ate) with no present but *esthio (ἐσθίω)* I eat (32).

mycteria Gr. snout or nose; *mycter (μυκτήρ)* snout; *mucterizo (μυκτηρίζω)* turn up the nose, be ironic (43).

myioparus Gr. closed tit; Jobling (2010, pp.263) reports name from Gr. *Muo (μύω)* to close and *parus* tit; refers to the covered nostrils by frontal plumes of the bird (54).

myoptilus Gr. mouse (coloured) plumage; *mys, myos (μῦς μυός)* mouse; *ptilon (πτίλον)* feather, plume (schoutedenapus, scarce swift, 230, 230,) T. Salvadori, 1888.

myrmecocichla Gr. ant thrush; *myrmex, myrmekos (μύρμηξ, μύρμηκος)* ant; *kichle or chikhla (κίχλη* or in modern Gr. *τσίχλα)* thrush (55).

N

nabouroup Namaqua name of the bird coined by Francois Levaillant (1753-1824) (onychognathus, pale-winged starling, 368, 960) F. M. Daudin, 1800.

naevius L. marked; *naevus* mole, birthmark, spot, blemish (coracias, purple roller, 242, 171) F. M. Daudin, 1800.

namaqua/namaquus from Namaqualand; Namaqualand is an arid region that part of it is in South Africa and the other part in Namibia; it is divided by the Orange river; Namaqua is also the name of the Khoikhoi people inhabiting the area (pterocles, namaqua sandgrouse, 198, 337, J. F. Gmelin, 1789) (dendropicos, bearded woodpecker, 258, 136, M. Lichtenstein, 1793).

namibornis Nama & Gr. bird of the Namib; *Namib* vast place in Nama; probably the only true desert in southern Africa, the Namib is a coastal desert that stretches more than 2,000 km along Namibia's Atlantic coast all the way into South Africa; *ornis* (ὄρνις) bird in ancient Gr. (54).

nanus Gr. dwarf; *nanos* (νάνος) dwarf. L. *nanus* derives from Gr. (turnix, black-rumped buttonquail, 132, 120) C. J. Sundevall, 1850.

narina from a Khoikhoi word for a flower; according to R. Lesson, Narina was the name of a beautiful Khoikhoi girl with a difficult name to pronounce or 'disagreeable to the ear' and Levaillant's mistress (apalotherma, narina trogon, 248, 166) J. F. Stephens, 1815.

nasutus L. long-nosed; *nasus* nose; *nasutus* having long nose (tockus, african grey hornbill, 246, 155) C. Linnaeus, 1766.

natalensis from Natal South Africa and Port Natal (Durban); when Vasco da Gama sailed by the coast of South Africa, looking for a way to India, at Christmas 1497 he named the area Natal; Portuguese *natal* chritmas, native; today it is called KwaZulu Natal (pternistis, natal spurfowl, 126, 72, A. Smith, 1833) (caprimulgus, swamp nightjar, 226, 268, A. Smith, 1845) (cossypha, red-capped robin-chat, 310, 932, A. Smith, 1840) (chloropeta, dark-capped yellow warbler, 320, 805, A. Smith, 1847) (cisticola, croaking cisticola, 332, 835, A. Smith, 1843).

naumanni after Johann Andreas *Naumann* (1744-1826), a German farmer and amateur naturalist; he wrote a book on the birds of Germany, *Naturgeschichte der Vogel Deutschlands* and he was the father of Johann Friedrich Naumann (1780-1857), artist and editor who was widely regarded as the founder of scientific ornithology in Europe, and who wrote *Die Eier der Vogel Deutchlands, in 1818* (Beolens & Watkins, 2005, pp. 248)(falco, lesser kestrel, 122, 545) J. G. Fleischer, 1818.

neafrapus Gr. new african legless (swift); *nea (νέα)* new; *afra (άφρα)* african; *apus (άπους)* legless, swift; *cypselus apous* of Aristotle (32).

nebularia L. cloydy, misty; *nebula* mist, fog, cloud, vapour, obscurity; Jobling (2010, pp. 266) reports *'Norwegian name Skoddefoll mist-foal, for the Common Greenshank, alluding to its misty, marshy habitat and supposed whinnying cries'* (tringa, common greenshank, 168, 354) J. E. Gunnerus, 1767.

necrosyrtes Gr. corpse-pulling; *necros (νεκρός)* dead, deceased, corpse; *syro (σύρω* or *serno σέρνω* in modern Gr.) drag, draw, pull (39).

nectarinia Gr. pertaining to nectar; *nectar (νέκταρ)* the drink of the Gods; since 1069 AD it is also used as the name of the sweet liquid found in flowers; one etymological suggestion is that it is the combination of *nec-ys (νέκυς)* dead and the sanskrit word *tárati* 'to cross' and it would mean 'to overcome death' (56).

neergaardi after P. *Neergaard,* a recruiting official for the Witwatersrand mines in s Mozambique, around 1907, who assisted C. H. B Grant on his expedition (cinnyris, neergard's sunbird, 376, 991) C. H. B. Grant, 1908.

neglectus L. neglected; *neglectus* disregarded, overlooked, neglected, ignored; *neglegere* to neglect, not care for, to overlook; probably because it was recently described (phalacrocorax, bank cormorant, 54, 577) J. A. Wahlberg, 1855.

neophron Gr. *neophron (νεόφρων)* new mind, new thinking; *neo (νέο)* new *phren, phrenos (φρήν, φρενός)* mind, thinking; in Gr. mythology, Aegypios was having an affair with Neophron's mother; Neophron, his friend, tricked Aegypios to sleep with his own mother; Zeus, the father of Gods, turned both former friends into vultures (39).

neotis Gr. new bustard; *neo (νέο)* new; otis *(ὠτίς, -ίδος)* bustard (34).

nereis Gr. Nereis, Nereides *(Νηρηίς, Νηρηίδες)* in Gr. mythology are the fifty sea-nymphs, friendly to sailors and often escorting Poseidon, the God of the sea, daughters of Nereus and Doris (garrodia, grey-backed storm-petrel, 48, 1142) J. Gould, 1841.

nesocichla *Gr. island thrush; nesos (νῆσος and in modern Gr. nesi νησί) island* (Tristan da Cunha); *kichle or cichla (κίχλη or in modern Gr. τσίχλα) thrush.*

nesospiza Gr. island finch; *nesos (νῆσος) island* (Tristan da Cunha); *spiza (σπίζα)* finch.

netta Gr. duck; *netta* or *nessa (νῆττα* or *νῆσσα)* duck (27).

nettapus Gr. duck foot; *netta* or *nessa (νῆττα* or *νῆσσα)* duck; *pous, podos (ποῦς, ποδός)* foot, leg; Jobling (2010, pp. 269) reports that the African pygmy goose was believed to have the feet and body of a duck and the bill and neck of a goose (27).

nicator Gr. conqueror, victorious; *nicator (νικάτωρ)* was the name of Seleucus I, king of Syria and the name of the Macedonian bodyguard (50).

nigra/niger L. black; *niger, -gra, -um* black, dark, unlucky (ciconia, black stork, 70, 620, C. Linnaeus, 1758) (chlidonias, black tern, 196, 471, C. Linnaeus, 1758) (parus, southern black tit, 290, 738, L. J. P. Vieillot, 1818) (bubalornis, red-billed buffalo-weaver, 382, 1003, A. Smith, 1836).

nigricans L. blackish, black or swarthy; *nigrare* to be black or to make black; *niger* black, dark, unlucky (pinarocorys, dusky lark, 260, 876, C. J. Sundevall, 1850) (pycnonotus, african red-eyed bulbul, 294, 767, L. J. P. Vieillot, 1818).

nigricapillus L. black haired or black-capped; *niger* black, dark, unlucky; *capillus* hair, hair of head, fur or wool of animals (lioptilus, bush blackcap, 294, 814, L. J. P. Vieillot, 1818).

nigricollis L. black-necked; *niger* black, dark, unlucky; *collum* neck, throat (podiceps, black-necked grebe, 60, 562) C. L. Brehm, 1831.

nigrifrons L. black forehead; *niger* black, dark, unlucky; *frons, -ontis* forehead, front, face, facade, appearance (telophorus, black-fronted bush-shrike, 362, 703) A. Reichenow, 1896.

nigrigenis L. & Gr. black-cheeked; *niger* black, dark, unlucky; Gr. *Genys, genyos (γένυς, γένυος)* cheek, jaw (agapornis, black-cheeked lovebird, 208, 229) W.L. Sclater, 1906.

nigripennis L. black-feathered, black-winged; *niger* black, dark, unlucky; *penna, pinna, -ae* feather, wing; Eng. *pen* (gallinago, african snipe, 172, 344) C. L. Bonaparte, 1839).

nilaus anagram of *Lanius,* genus of true shrikes (47).

nilotica of the Nile; the Nile. Arabic النيل. L. Nilus; Gr. Νεῖλος; regarded the longest river in the world, it crosses eleven countries; the two major tributaries, the blue and the white, meet close to the capital of Sudan Khartoum; the White Nile comes from the Great Lake area in central Africa while the Blue Nile comes from lake Tana in Ethiopia (sterna, gull-billed tern 190, 449) J. F. Gmelin, 1789.

nipalensis from Nepal; Nipal is Nepal; Nepali नेपाल; a holy man named 'Ne' came to Kathmandu, and Nepal means 'place protected by Ne' from the Pali word 'pala', according to a local legend (aquila, steppe eagle, 94, 528) B. H. Hodgson, 1833.

nitens L. shining, bright, glittering; *nitere* shine, glitter, look bright, bloom, thrive (lamprotornis, cape glossy starling, 366, 963) C. Linnaeus, 1766.

nitidula L. relatively bright, shining; *nitidus* shining, bright, blooming (lagonosticta, brown firefinch, 402, 1062, G. Hartlaub, 1886) (mandingoa, green twinspot, 400, 1045, G. Hartlaub, 1865).

nivea L. snowy; *niveus* snowy, covered with snow, white; *nix, nivis* snow, flake, whiteness, coldness (pagodroma, snow petrel, 32) G. Forster, 1777.

niveoguttatus L. white-spotted; *niveus* snowy, covered with snow, white; *nix, nivis* snow, flake, whiteness, coldness; *gutta* drop, spot, speck (hypargos, red-throated twinspot, 400, 1056) W. Peters, 1868.

nordmanni after Alexander Davidovich von *Nordmann* (1803-1866), a Finnish Professor of Zoology at Odessa and collector of natural history specimens in Southern Russia; he later became Professor at the University of Helsinki (glareola, black-winged pranticole, 176, 429) G. Fischer von Waldheim, 1842.

notata L. marked, spotted; *nota* mark, sign, note, letter, tattoo-mark; *notare* to mark, to observe, to brand, to inscribe; the common name of the bird, Knysna, is a Khoikhoi word that probably means 'ferns' and is a town in the Western Cape Province in South Africa (campethera, knysna woodpecker, 258, 132) M. Lichtenstein, 1823.

nubicoides resembling nubicus (northern carmine bee-eater *merops nubicus* of the Sahel region; Arabic *sāḥil* ساحل shore, coast; *Nubia* Nubia; -*oides* Gr. ending that means resembling; from Nubia, a region along the Nile in Southern Egypt and Northern Sudan; the name derives from the Noba people (merops, southern carmine bee-eater, 240, 195) M. A. P. OE. Des Murs & J. Pucheran 1846.

nuchalis L. nucha nape, referring to the nuchal collar; *nucha* nape,

back of neck from Arabic *nukha* (نخاع) marrow (glareola, rock pranticole, 176, 430) G. R. Gray, 1849.

numenius Gr. new moon, referring to crescent shaped bills; *neo (νέο)* new; *mene (μήνη)* moon Eng. *meniscus; men,-nos (μήν, μηνός)* month, *menas (μήνας)* month in modern Gr.; Hesychius mentions the bird *noumenios*; Eng. *meno*pause, *men*struation (36).

numida after Numidia, an ancient kingdom in North west Africa; Greeks called the people living in the area west of Carthage *Nomads (νομάδες)* and that became *Numidae* in Latin (26).

nyassae after Nyassa District in former German East Africa, now Tanzania, or Nyasaland, now Malawi or lake Nyasa, one of the Great Lakes in Africa, almost 580 km long; it is divided between three countries and it was named by David Livingstone in 1859; the first European to see it though was Candido José da Costa Cardoso, a Portuguese trader in 1846 (anthus, wood pipit, 350, 1110) O. R. Neumann, 1906.

nycticorax Gr. raven or crow of the night, because at night its voice is cacophonous; *nyx, nyctos (νύξ, νυκτός)* night; *korax, korakos (κόραξ, κόρακος)* raven or crow; Jobling (2009, pp. 277) reports the bird of evil omen mentioned by Aristotle and other authors (nycticorax, black-crowned night-heron, 68, 597) C. Linnaeus, 1758.

O

obtusa L. blunt; *obtusus,-a* blunt, stupid; *obtundere* to make blunt, strike, beat, deafen; *ob + tundere;* probably referring to the shape of its tail; Eng. obtuse (vidua, broad-tailed paradise-wydah, 392, 1071) J. Chapin, 1922.

occipitalis L. of back of the head; *occipitium,-ii* or *occiput, -itis* the back of the head; *ob + caput; caput* head, edge, top; Eng. occipital lobe, occipital bone (aegypius, white-headed vulture, 86, 492, W. J. Burchell, 1824) (lophaetus, long-crested eagle, 98, 539, F. M. Daudin, 1800).

oceanicus Gr. oceanic, of the ocean; oceanos *(ὠκεανός)* ocean; in Gr. mythology Oceanus

(Ὠκεανός) was a Titan and a river that surrounded the earth without springs or mouth; the common name commemorates Alexander Wilson (1766-1813), an American who wrote the American Ornithology and is considered by many the Father of American Ornithology; his accurate descriptions and superb illustrations are noted (oceanites, wilson's storm-petrel, 46, 635) H. Kuhl, 1820.

oceanites Gr. of the ocean; after Oceanus *(Ὠκεανός)* or his three thousand daughters, sea nymphs and river protectors, the Oceanids *(Ὠκεανίδες)* (45).

oceanodroma Gr. ocean runner; *oceanos (ὠκεανός)* ocean; *dromos (δρόμος)* road race in ancient Gr.; in modern Gr. it means road (45).

ochropus Gr. yellow-footed; ochre *(ὤχρα)* ochre, yellow colour; *ochros (ὠχρός)* pale, pallid or yellow; *pous,* podos *(ποῦς, ποδός)* foot or leg; *podi (πόδι)* in modern Gr. (tringa, green sandpiper, 166, 357) C. Linnaeus, 1758, Conrad Gesner 1555.

ocularis L. of the eye; *oculus* eye; refers to markings around the eye; Eng. ocular, oculist (ploceus, spectacled weaver, 384, 1011) A. Smith, 1828.

oena Gr. *oenas* a wild pigeon; *oenas,-ados* (οἰνάς,-άδος) vineyard, wine, wild pigeon that has the colour of mature grapes; *oenos (οἶνος)* wine (34)

oenanthe Gr. wine-flower; *oenanthe (οἰνάνθη)* the first sprout of vineyard; *oenos (οἶνος)* wine; *anthos (ἄνθος)* flower; it was this or another bird that Greeks called wine-flower because it returned to Greece when gapevines blossom in spring; its common name was *white arse* (referring to its white rump) and censorship (bowdlerisation) changed it to wheatear (oenanthe, northern wheatear, 304, 949) C. Linnaeus, 1758

olivacea /olivaceus L. olive-green; *oliva, -ae* olive, olive tree, olive branch (cyanomitra, olive sunbird, 378, 979, A. Smith 1840) (geocolaptes, ground woodpecker, 256, 134, J. F. Gmelin, 1788) (stactolaema, green barbet, 252, 140, G. E. Shelley, 1880) (telophorus, olive bush-shrike, 362, 702, Shaw, 1809) (turdus, olive thrush, 298, 907, C. Linnaeus, 1766).

olivaceiceps L. olive-headed; *oliva, -ae* olive, olive tree, olive branch; *-ceps (caput,-itis)* head, top, edge (ploceus, olive-headed weaver, 386, 1021) A. Reichenow, 1899.

olivetorum of the olive groves; *oliva, -ae* olive, olive tree, olive branch; *olivetum* olive grove (hippolais, olive-tree warbler, 314, 803) H. E. Strickland, 1837.

onocrotalus Gr. pelican; *onos (ὄνος)* donkey; *krotalon (κρόταλον)* musical instrument made of two pieces of cane, ceramic or metal, used in Cybele's (the mother goddess from Anatolia) worship (pelecanus, great white pelican, 58, 614) C. Linnaeus, 1758.

onychognathus Gr. claw-like jaws; *onyx, onychos (ὄνυξ, ὄνυχος)* claw, nail, talon; *gnathos (γνάθος)* jaw (55).

onychoprion Gr claw saw; *onyx, onychos (ὄνυξ, ὄνυχος)* claw, nail, talon; *prion, prionos (πρίων, πρίονος)* saw; ancient Gr. *prio (πρίω)* to cut, to saw (formerly *sterna*, 194).

oreophilais Gr. mountain-loving; *oros (ὄρος)* mountain; *philos (φίλος)* loving, friend

Eng. <u>philos</u>ophy wisdom-loving, <u>phil</u>anthropist people-loving etc. (52).

orientalis L. of the east, eastern; *oriens,-tis* rising sun, east (psalidoprocne, eastern saw-wing, 280, 765) A. Reichenow, 1889.

oriolus L. golden, yellow; probably from *aureolus* golden, beautiful, splendid; *aurum* gold, golden item, jewel (oriolus, eurasian golden oriole, 286, 680) C. Linnaeus, 1758.

orix Gr. rice; Roberts suggests the name refers to the bird's habit to feed in rice paddies; Gr. *oryza (ὄρυζα)* is the same word in L. and derives from the East Persian word *vrize* and sanskrit *vrihi;* in modern Gr. rice is *ryzi (ρύζι)* (euplectes, southern red bishop, 388, 1028) C. Linnaeus, 1758.

ortygospiza Gr. quail-finch; *ortyx, ortygos (ὄρτυξ, ὄρτυγος* and *ortyki ορτύκι* in modern Gr.) quail; *spiza (σπίζα)* finch (57).

ostralegus Gr. and L. oyster-gatherer; *ostreion (ὄστρειον* or *ὄστρεον)* L. *ostreum* or *ostrea* oyster; L. *legere* to gather, to pick (haematopus, eurasian oystercatcher, 150, 389) C. Linnaeus, 1758.

otus Gr. an eared owl; *otos (ὦτος* or *ὠτός)* long-eared owl, horn-owl (33).

ovampensis from Ovampo river; Ovampoland or Ovamboland is the area where the largest ethnic group of Namibia, the Ovambo (or Ambo) live, at the north part of the country with a number living in neighbouring Angola (accipiter, ovampo sparrowhawk, 110,517) J. H. Gurney Sr, 1875.

oxyura Gr. sharp tail; *oxya (ὀξεῖα) sharp;* oura *(οὐρά)* tail (27).

P

pachycoccyx Gr. thick cuckoo or thick rump; *pachys pacheos (παχύς παχέος)* thick, dense, large, having lots of fat; *coccyx κόκκυξ* cuckoo or rump, the last bone of the spine, from the sound of the cuckoo *kokky,* also used by humans as a an exclamation meaning *come on! fast!;* cuckoo was Hera's sacred bird (31).

pachyptila Gr. thick-feathered; *pachys pacheos (παχύς, παχέος)* thick, dense, large, having lots of fat; *ptilon* (πτίλον) feather, plume, plumage (46).

pacificus L. of the Pacific Ocean; the largest ocean in the world, almost one third of the surface of the earth; it was named Mar Pacífico by Ferdinand Magellan and its name means 'peaceful sea'; *pacificus* peaceful; *pacificare* make peace; *pax, pacis* peace, harmony (puffinus, wedge-tailed shearwater, 40, 674) J. F. Gmelin, 1789.

paena probably from Tswana; Jobling (2010, pp. 288) suggests the name *Phena* or *Phene* for this bird; its common name refers to the Kalahari desert, a vast semi arid area in southern Africa; from Tswana *kgala* 'the great thirst' or *kgalagadi* 'a waterless place' (cercotrichas, kalahari scrub-robin, 308, 940) A. Smith, 1836.

pagodroma Gr. ice runner; *pagos* πάγος ice, frost, sea-ice; *dromos* (δρόμος) road, route, path, course, race, run; *dromeas* (δρομέας) runner, racer; *petrel* from Peter the Apostle; refers to the bird looking like it walks on water; *Peter* is from Gr. *petros* (πέτρος) rock.

pallidiventris L. pale belly; *pallidus* pale, pallid, greenish; *pallere* to be pale or yellow, to faint; *venter ventris* stomach, belly, womb (parus, cinnamon-breasted tit, 290 (Roberts, 2009, treats it as a subspecies of *parus rufiventris* pp. 740) J. V. Barbosa du Bocage, 1877.

pallidus L. pallid, pale; *pallidus* pale, pallid, greenish; *pallere* to be pale or yellow, to faint; the white eye's common name refers to the Orange River, the longest river in South Africa; it was named after the Dutch Royal House; it rises in the Drakensberg and flows in the Atlantic Ocean; it is also known as Gariep River, Groote River or Senqu River (apus, pallid swift, 228, 238, G. E. Shelley, 1870) (bradornis, pale flycatcher, 342, 910, J. W. von Müller, 1851) (charadrius, chestnut-banded plover, 154, 401, H. E. Strickland, 1852) (zosterops, orange river white-eye, 344, 823, W. J. Swainson, 1838).

palpebrata L. with eyelids, '*referring to prominent white eye crescents*' (Roberts, 2009); *palpebra* eyelid; *palpare* stroke, coax, flatter, wheedle (phoebetria, light-mantled albatross, 30, 653) J. R. Forster, 1785.

paludicola L. marsh dweller; *palus,-udis* marsh or pool; *paluster* marshy; *cola* inhabitant; *colere* to dwell, inhabit, live in (riparia, brown-throated martin, 282, 744,) L. J. P. Vieillot, 1817.

paludipasser L. marsh-sparrow; p*alus,-udis* marsh or pool; *paluster* marshy; *passer* sparrow (57).

palustris L. marshy, swampy; *palus,-udis* marsh or pool; *paluster, palustris* marshy. (acrocephalus, marsh warbler, 318, 798) J. M. Bechstein, 1798.

pammelaina Gr. all black; *pan-* παν- all, everything (the n of *pan* turns to m when followed by a word that begins with m); *melas melaina (f)* μέλας μέλαινα black, dark; *pan*-orama, *melanine* (melaenornis, southern black flycatcher, 340, 915) E. S. Stanley, 1814.

pandion *Pandion (Πανδίων)* was the name of two legendary kings of Athens, the fifth and eighth in succession, and also a hero of Athens who may have been one of the kings; none of them was turned into a bird of prey or any other kind of bird (39).

papua from Papua, New Guinea; *Papua* is the second largest island in the world and belongs to two countries: Papua New Guinea and Indonesia; there are several proposals for the origin of the name Papua: in Tidore it would mean 'not united', in Malay 'frizzly haired' and in Biak 'the land below'; the penguin was erroneously reported to be in Papua by Sonnerat, who had actually never vsited it! (Jobling, 2010, pp. 291) (pygoscelis, gentoo penguin, 18, 630) J. R. Forster, 1781.

paradisea/paradiseus ancient Persian *pardez*, meaning walled garden and Greek *paradeisos (παράδεισος)* used by Xenophon, meant parks with wild animals; it later came to mean paradise; Roberts hints it could suggest resemblance to angels (anthropoides, blue crane 142,309, A. A. H. Lichtenstein, 1793) (vidua, Long-tailed paradise wydah, 392, 1073, C. Linnaeus, 1758) (sterna, arctic tern, 192, 460, E. Pontoppidan, 1763).

parasiticus Gr. parasitic; he who lives on somebody else's expense; *para (παρα-)* next to, too much, despite, exaggeration; *sitos (σῖτος)* wheat; *sition (σιτίον)* food; *sitizo (σιτίζω)* to feed; the original meaning was of someone who eats at somebody else's table and tries to pay back with exaggerated praises and flattery (stercorarius, parasitic jaeger, 182, 435) C. Linnaeus, 1758.

parisoma L & Gr. tit's body; L. *parus* tit (*parum* too little, not enough); *soma (σῶμα)* body (51).

parus L. tit; *parus* tit; *parus* equal, like, suitable; *parum* too little, not enough (49).

parvus L. small; *parvus* small, little, slight, cheap, unimportant; comparative *minor;* superlative *minimus* (cypsiurus, african palm-swift, 230, 233) M. H. C. Lichtenstein, 1823.

passer L. sparrow; *passer* sparrow (58).

passerina L. sparrow-like, sparrow-sized; its common name is Gr. and it means one tone i.e. dull voice (mirafra, monotonous lark, 266, 860) N. C. G. F. Gyldenstolpe, 1926.

patagonicus from Patagonia; *Patagonia* is a region in South America shared by Chile and Argentina; it was named by Ferdinand Magellan in 1520 who used the word *patagón* for the people of the area; he thought they were giants; it was probably the Tehuelches, a tribe of quite tall people but not the giants reported for centuries by imaginative European sailors! (aptenodytes, king penguin, 18, 629) J. F. Miller, 1778.

pavo L. peacock; *pavo* peacock (26).

pectoralis L. of the breast or pertaining to the breast; *pectus pectoris* breast, heart (caprimulgus, fiery-necked nightjar, 224, 264, G. Cuvier, 1817) (circaetus, black-chested snake-eagle, 92, 493, A. Smith, 1829) (coracina, white-breasted cuckooshrike, 284, 732 W. Jardine & Selby, 1828) (malcorus, rufous-eared warbler, 336, 849, A. Smith, 1829).

pecuarius L. a grazer, of cattle; *pecu* cattle, flocks, beast, pastures, money; *pecuarius* of sheep or cattle, cattle breeder; its common name refers to Friedrich Heinrich Freiher von Kittlitz (1799-1874), a German artist, naval officer, explorer and ornithologist; he went to North Africa, with his friend Eduard Rüppell and later sailed round the world and wrote *Twenty-Four Views of the Vegetation of the Coasts and Islands of the Pacific* in 1861 (Beolens & Watkins, 2003, pp. 189) (charadrius, kittlitz's plover, 152, 398) C. J. Temminck, 1823.

pelagicus Gr. of the sea, marine; *pelagos (πέλαγος)* sea, open sea; archi-*pelago* (hydrobates, european storm-petrel, 46, 638) C. Linnaeus, 1758.

pelagodroma Gr. sea-runner; *pelagos πέλαγος* sea, open sea; *dromos (δρόμος)* road, route, path, course, race, run; *dromeas (δρομέας)* runner, racer (45).

pelecanoides Gr. resembling a pelecan; *pelekanos (πελεκάνος)* pelican; *-oides (-οειδές)* resembling (43).

pelecanus Gr. a pelican; *pelekanos (πελεκάνος)* pelican; *pelekys (πέλεκυς)* axe; refers to the use of the bird's beak (43).

peli after Hendrik Severinus *Pel* (1818-1876), the Dutch governor of the Gold Coast (now Ghana) between 1840-1850; he was an amateur naturalist but also acted as a trained taxidermist for the Dutch State Museum of Natural History; the year he described the bird, 1851, he also published *Over de jagt aan de Goudkust, volgens eene tienjarige eigene ondervinding* (Beolens & Watkins, 2003, pp, 265) (scotopelia, pel's fishing owl, 222, 259) C. L. Bonaparte, 1850.

peliperdix Gr. bruised or grey partridge; *pelios* bruised; *refers to heavily barred or blotched underparts; peleia (πέλεια)* the wild pigeon *Columba oenas* thus named because of its dark colour; *peleiai (πέλειαι)* priestesses that could foresee the future as did the magic pigeons of Dodoni; *pelios (πελιός)* bruised; *Pelias*, king of Iolkos, was named after the dark mark he had on his face, by a horse kick when he was deserted with his twin brother, *Neleas*, by their mother; *perdix (πέρδιξ) (perdika πέρδικα* in modern Gr.) partridge; *perdomai πέρδομαι* to fart, to break wind; refers to the sound of the bird's wings when alarmed! (26).

peltata Gr. with a light shield; *refers to wattle around eye* (Roberts, 2009, pp. 719) *pelte (πέλτη)* light shield, half-moon shaped made of tree branches and covered by goat skin; L. pelta; Gr. *peltastes (πελταστής)* warrior carrying a light shield and spear (platysteira, black-throated wattle-eye, 346, 719) C. J. Sundevall, 1850.

pennatus L. feathered, *in reference to feathered tarsi* (Roberts, 2009); *penna, -ae* feather, wing, flight; Eng. *pen* (aquila, booted eagle, 98, 535) J. F. Gmelin, 1788.

percnopterus Gr. dark or dusky-winged; *perknos (περκνός)* dark, dusky, especially for riping grapes or olives; *pteron (πτερόν)* (*ftero* φτερό in modern Gr) wing (neophron, egyptian vulture, 88, 485) C. Linnaeus, 1758.

peregrinus L. wanderer, stranger; many of these birds migrate, hence the name; *peregrinus* strange, foreign, alien, exotic, a non Roman in Rome, non Roman; *peregre* away from home, abroad; Eng. *peregrine* (falco, peregrine falcon, 116, 557) Marmaduke Tunstall, 1771.

perlatum L. wearing pearls; *perla* pearl (medieval L.) (glaucidium, pearl-spotted owlet, 220, 261) L. J. P. Vieillot, 1818.

pernis Gr. kind of hawk, probably a corruption of *pternis*

(πτέρνις) kind of hawk, Aristotle Z, hist. 9. 36. 1 (39).

perreini after Jean *Perrein* (1750-1805), a French naturalist and collector who travelled to northern Africa, Arabia, Persia, India and North America; he died of malaria (Beolens & Watkins, 2003, pp. 267) (estrilda, grey waxbill, 396, 1049) L. J. P. Vieillot, 1817.

persicus from Persia; a country in Asia, now known as Iran, home of one of the oldest civilizations in the world; the West called the country Persia until 1935 from ancient Greek *Persis* (Περσίς) land of the Persians (merops, blue-cheeked bee-eater, 238, 191) P. S. Pallas, 1773.

petronia Gr. to do with rocks; *petra (πέτρα)* rock, stone; *petros (πέτρος)* a rock used by fighters; *local Bolognese (Italian) name for the rock sparrow* (Jobling, 2010, pp. 300) (58).

phaeopus Gr. grey-footed; *phaeos (φαιός)* dusky, brown, grey; *pous, podos (πούς, ποδός)* foot (numenius, common whimbrel, 170, 349) C. Linnaeus, 1758.

phaethon Gr. shining, radiant; *phaetho (φαέθω)* to shine; Phaethon in Gr. mythology was the son of the Sun, known for the accident he had when he tried to lead the horses of the Sun and was struck down by Apollo; it was also the name of one of the four horses of Eos *('Ηώς),* goddess of dawn; it was also the name of Eos' son and the planet Jupiter; alluding *to tropical distribution, following the path of the sun* (Roberts, 2009) (41).

phalacrocorax Gr. cormorant, literally bald raven; *phalakros (φαλακρός)* bald-headed; *korax, korakos (κόραξ, κόρακος)* raven, crow; *phalaros (φάλαρος)* white or partly white (42).

phalaropus Gr. coot feet; *referring to lobed toes* (Roberts, 2009) *phalaris, phalaridos (φαλαρίς φαλαρίδος)* coot; *pous, podos (ποῦς, ποδός)* foot; the coot takes its name due to its bald head; *phalakros (φαλακρός)* bald-headed; *phalaros φάλαρος* white or partly white (36).

phedina combination probably of Gr. *phaeos φαιός* dusky, grey; and either *tsidisidina* Malagasy for martin (Roberts) or Italian *rondine* swallow (Jobling, 2010, pp. 302) (49).

philetairus Gr. loving companion; *philos (φίλος)* loving, fond of, friend; *(ἑταῖρος)* companion, friend, comrade (in arms); *philo-*sophy, *phila-*telist, *Phil*ip (56).

philomachus Gr. battle loving, pugnacious, martial; *in reference to elaborate lek displays* (Roberts, 2009); *philos (φίλος)* loving, fond of, friend; *mache (μάχη)* battle, combat, fight; *machomai (μάχομαι)* to fight (36).

phoebastria Gr. fortune-teller, prophetess; *phoibastria (φοιβάστρια)* diviner, soothsayer, fortune-teller, prophetess; *phoibao (φοιβάω)* to clean, to touch; *phoibos (φοῖβος)* clear, transparent, bright and a name for Apollo, the god of the sun (45).

phoebetria Gr. purifier; *phoibetria (φοιβήτρια)* purifier, expiator; *phoibao (φοιβάω)* to clean, to touch; *phoibos (φοῖβος)* clear, transparent, bright and a name for Apollo, the god of the sun (45).

phoenicopterus Gr. flamingo; *phoenicoptero (φοινικόπτερο)* flamingo, red-winged; literally the wings of a phoenix or red wings; *phoenix, phoenikos (φοῖνιξ, φοίνικος)* red, purple, scarlet, crimson; mythological bird said to live 500 years and when it sensed death nearing it burned in a fire and was reborn from the ashes; *Phoenicians (Phoenikes Φοίνικες* in Gr.) were a people that the Greeks called them so and it meant red, purple or scarlet, probably meaning 'not white' and not because they used to be producers of 'purple dye'as it was earlier suggested; *pteron (πτερόν)* wing (43).

phoeniculus Gr. scarlet; diminutive of Phoenix (See phoenicopterus above) (29).

phoenicurus Gr. scarlet-tailed; (See phoenicopterus above); *oura (οὐρά)* tail (phoenicurus, common redstart, 306, 945) C. Linnaeus, 1758.

phragmacia Gr. *'The generic name which is feminine and formed from the botanical genera Phragmites and Acacia, two principal plant constituents of its usual habitat'* (Brooke & Dean 1990 at Jobling, 2010, pp. 304); *phragmites (φραγμίτης)* the common reed; *phragma (φράγμα)* barrier, dam; *phraktes (φράκτης)* hedge; *akakia (ἀκακία)* acacia; *akakia (ἀκακία)* innocence, lack of malice (52).

phyllastrephus Gr. to bend or toss a leaf; *'referring to habit of scratching about in leaf litter'* (Roberts, 2009); *phyllon (φύλλον) (φύλλο* in modern Gr.) leaf; *strepho (στρέφω)* to turn, to bend, to toss (50).

phylloscopus Gr. leaf seeker; *'referring to leaf-gleaning behaviour'* (Roberts, 2009); *phyllon (φύλλον) (φύλλο* in modern Gr.) leaf; *scopos (σκοπός)* he who watches, guard (51).

picta L. painted; *picta* coloured, painted, tatooed; *pingere* to paint, embroider, to colour (ispidina, african pygmy-kingfisher, 234, 176) P. Boddaert, 1783.

pileata L. capped; *pilleatus* wearing the cap; *pileus* or *pilleus* a kind of Phrygian cap as a symbol of freedom; freed slaves used to wear a cap (oenanthe, capped wheatear, 304, 950) J. F. Gmelin, 1789.

pinarocorys Gr. dirty lark; *pinaros (πιναρός)* dirty, grimy, squalid; *korys, korythos (κόρυς, κόρυθος)* helmet made of copper, casque; *corysso (κορύσσω)* to put on a helmet; lark (53).

pinarornis Gr. dirty bird; Roberts says it refers to sooty plumage; *pinaros (πιναρός)* dirty, grimy, squalid; *ornis (ὄρνις)* bird in ancient Gr. (55).

pipiens L. chirping, peeping; *pipire* or *pipiare* to chirp, to pipe (cisticola, chirping cisticola, 334, 833) H. Lynes, 1930.

pipixcan *presumably from the Spanish apipizca, meaning 'gull'* (Roberts, 2009); Jobling (2010, pp. 308) says *it is the name given to a gull by Mexican Indians, according to Hernandez*; the common name of the bird refers to Rear-Admiral Sir John *Franklin* (1786-1847), a Brittish Naval officer and Arctic explorer; he served as lieutenant-governor of Tasmania (then Van Diemen's island) and disappeared in his last expedition (larus, franklin's gull, 186, 447) J. G. Wagler, 1831.

pitta *'Telugu Dravidian name pitta pretty bauble or pet; based on 'Bréve' of de Buffon'* (Jobling, 2010. pp. 308) Telugu is a language spoken in India and belongs to the Dravidian family of Indian languages (46).

platalea *'L. the Spoonbil P. leucorodia; name used by Cicero (106-43 BC)'* (Roberts, 2009); *platos* width, breadth; *platys, plateia (πλατύς, πλατεῖα)* wide, broad, flat; *lea* or *leia (λέα λεῖα)* smooth; Eng. *plate* (43).

platyrynchos Gr. flat-billed; *platys (πλατύς)* wide, broad, flat; *rhynchos (ρύγχος)* bill, snout (anas, mallard, 82, 106) C. Linnaeus, 1758.

platysteira Gr. *'broad or flat keel of a ship, referring to shape of bill'* (Roberts, 2009); *platys (πλατύς)* wide, broad, flat; *steira (στεῖρα)* keel of a ship (48).

plectropterus Gr. spurwing; *plektron (πλῆκτρον)* cock's spur; *pteron (πτερόν)* (*ftero φτερό* in modern Gr) wing; *'referring to carpal spur'* (Roberts, 2009) (27).

plegadis Gr. a sickle; *plegas, plegados (πληγάς, πληγάδος)* sickle (43).

pleschanka *'Russian name pleschanka for the Pied Wheatear (plesch (плешь) bald spot on the head)'* (Jobling, 2010, pp. 310); *'referring to white crown'* (Roberts, 2009) (oenanthe, pied wheatear, 304, 950) I. I. Lepechin, 1770.

plocepasser Gr. & L. weaver-sparrow; Gr. *ploceus (πλοκεύς)* weaver, braider, plaiter; *pleko (πλέκω)* to weave, to plait, to entwine; L. *passer* sparrow (56).

ploceus Gr. weaver; *ploceus (πλοκεύς)* weaver, braider, plaiter; *pleko πλέκω* to weave, to plait, to entwine (57).

plumatus L. feathered, plumed; *pluma* soft feather, fluff; *'with reference to crested forehead'* (Roberts, 2009) (prionops, white-crested helmet-shrike, 364, 707) G. Shaw, 1809.

plumbeus L. of lead, leaden grey; *plumbeus* of lead, heavy, dull; *plumbum* lead (myioparus, grey tit-flycatcher, 340, 922) G. Hartlaub, 1858.

plumosus L. feathered, plumed; *pluma* soft feather, fluff; (pinarornis, boulder chat, 292, 959) R. B. Sharpe, 1876.

pluvialis L. of rain; *pluvia* rain; *pluere* to rain; name refers to flocking and calling before rain (37).

podica Gr. of the foot; *pous, podos (ποῦς, ποδός)* foot; *'referring to the strange lobed toes'* (Roberts, 2009) (35).

podiceps L. rump-footed; *podex, podicis* rump, anus; *pes* foot; *'a reference to the legs being positioned far back on the body'* (Roberts, 2009) (41).

pogoniulus Gr. *diminutive of bearded; pogon, pogonos (πώγων, πώγωνος) beard, chin (28).*

pogonocichla Gr. bearded thrush; *pogon pogonos (πώγων, πώγωνος)* beard, chin; *kikhle (κίχλη)* thrush (*chichla τσίχλα* thrush in modern Gr.) *'pehaps referring to white throat spot'* (Roberts, 2009) (54).

poicephalus Gr. grey-headed; Jobling (2010, pp. 312) claims *poi* from *phaios* grey, dusky ; *cephale (κεφαλή)* head; could be from *poio (ποιῶ)* to make, so it would mean made of head (31).

polemaetus Gr. martial eagle; *polemos (πόλεμος)* war, fight, struggle, battle; *aetos (ἀετός)* eagle, king of birds (40).

polihierax Gr. grey hawk; *polios (πολιός)* sub-white, black and white, grey-haired; *hierax hierakos (ἱέραξ, ἱέρακος)* falcon, hawk; *iemai (ἵεμαι)* to assault, to swoop down on (41).

poliocephalus Gr. grey-headed; sub-white, black and white, grey-haired; *cephale (κεφαλή* ancient) head (cuculus, lesser cuckoo, 212, 209) J. Latham, 1790.

polyboroides Gr. resembling polyborus (*polyborus plancus* crested caracara); *poly (πολύ)* much, a lot; *bora (βορά)* the food of animals, devouring, eating; *-oides (-οειδες)* resembling (40).

pomarina/pomarinus the eagle is from Pomerania, an area by the Baltic sea, now divided between Germany and Poland; its name is from Slavic and means *'by the sea'*, po (по=next) + more (море=sea); the jaeger's name means nostril cover; *poma (πῶμα)* cover; *rhis rhinos (ρίς, ρινός)* nose, nostrils; from this word derives the name of *rhino*ceros horn on nose, and of course oto*rhino*laryngologist! (aquila, lesser spotted eagle, 94, 530, C. L. Brehm, 1831) (stercorarius, pomarine jaeger, 182, 434 C. J. Temminck, 1815).

porphyreolophus Gr. deep red-crested; *porphyra (πορφύρα)* a sea snail, the colouring substance from a number of sea snails of the genus *murex,*

imperial dye, royal purple, deep red; *lofio (λοφίο)* crest (gallirex, purple-crested turaco, 210, 248) N. A. Vigors, 1831.

porphyrio Gr. deep-red, purple; *porphyra (πορφύρα)* a sea snail, the colouring substance from a number of sea snails of the genus *murex*, imperial dye, royal purple, deep red; *porphyrion (πορφυρίων)* a bird mentioned by Aristophanes in Birds (707) and Aristotle (35).

porzana *'Local Venetian names porzana, sforzana and sporzana for the smaller crakes'* (Jobling, 2010, pp. 315) (porzana, spotted crake, 138, 328) C. Linnaeus, 1766.

pratincola L. meadow dweller; *pratum, prati* meadow, grass; *incola* inhabitant, resident, dweller, citizen; *incolere* inhabit, to live in, reside, sojourn (glareola, collared pratincole, 176, 427) C. Linnaeus, 1766.

prinia Javanese name *prinya* for the bar-winged prinia; a language spoken in central and east Java (52).

prionops Gr. saw-eyed; *prion (πρίων)* saw; *ops (ὤψ)* eye; *'refers to ragged fleshy eye wattles'* (Roberts, 2009) (48).

pririt French name given by Levaiilant, immitating its call-notes (Jobling, 2010, pp. 316) or *possibly to sounds of wing-fripping* (Roberts, 2009) (batis, pririt batis, 346, 718) L. J. P. Vieillot, 1818.

procellaria L. bird of the storm; *procella, -ae* storm, rage, tumult, raid (46).

prodotiscus Gr. little betrayer; diminutive of *prodotes (προδότης)* betrayer, informer, traitor; *prodido (προ+δίδω=*give) to betray (28).

progne Gr. Progne or Procne; Procne was the daughter of the king of Athens, Pandion; she married the king of Thrace, Tereas; they soon had a son, Itys; Tereas raped Procne's sister Philomela and cut her tongue; Philomela sent her sister a tapestry with the whole incident depicted; Procne's revenge was terrible; she killed her son and fed him to his father; she fled with her sister to avoid Tereas' wrath and the two sisters were turned into birds by Zeus; Philomela became a nightingale and Procne a swallow (euplectes, long-tailed widowbird, 390, 1035) P. Boddaert, 1783.

promerops Gr. related or close to bee-eaters; *pro (προ)* close to, similar; *merops (μέροψ)* bee-eater; *merops* was used in poetry to signify articulated people, people who divided voices (56).

psalidoprocne Gr. scissors swift or swallow; *psalis, psalidos (ψαλίς, ψαλίδος)* scissors; *'reference to barbed edges of outer primaries'* (Roberts, 2009); Progne or Procne (see progne above) (49).

pseudalethe Gr. false *Alethe*; *pseudos (ψευδός)* false, not true, lying; *Alethe* ; alethes *(ἀληθής)* true, not covered, sincere (54).

pseudhirundo Gr. & L. false swallow; Gr. *pseudos (ψευδός)* false, not true, lying; L. *hirundo* swallow (49).

pseudosimilis Gr. & L. false similis; Gr. *pseudos (ψευδός)* false, not true, lying; *similis 'referring to Long-billed pipit'* (Roberts, 2009) (anthus, kimberley pipit, 350, 1110) R. Liversidge & G. Voelker, 2002.

psittacula Gr. small parrot; diminutive of *psittakos (ψιττακός)* parrot (32).

psophocichla Gr. noisy thrush; *psophos (ψόφος)* noise; *kikhle (κίχλη)* thrush (*cichla τσίχλα* thrush in modern Gr.) (54).

pternistis Gr. one who strikes or trips with the heel; 'referring to double spurs of male' (Roberts, 2009); *pterne (πτέρνη)* heel; *pterna (πτέρνα)* or *fterna (φτέρνα)* in modern Gr.; *pternister (πτερνιστήρ)* spur (26).

pterocles Gr. noted for the wing; *pteron πτερόν (ftero φτερό* in modern Gr) wing; *-cles* derives from *cleos (κλέος)* glory (35).

pterodroma Gr. winged runner; *pteron (πτερόν) (ftero φτερό* in modern Gr) wing; *dromos (δρόμος)* running competition; road in modern Gr.; 'referring to swift flight' (Roberts, 2009) (46).

ptilopsis Gr. feathered appearance; *ptilon (πτίλον)* feather, plume, plumage; *opsis (ὄψις)* appearance or face (33).

puffinus 'English name Puffin, originally applied to the cured carcass of the fat nestling shearwater, a delicacy until the end of the 18ᵗʰ century. By confusion and association the name was gradually also applied to the puffin Fratercula, becoming fixed on that species during the second half of the 19ᵗʰ century, but retained in ornithology for the shearwaters' (Lockwood, 1984 at Jobling, 2009, pp. 323) (puffinus, manx shearwater, 42, 675) M. T. Brünnich, 1764.

pugnax L. battle loving, pugnacious, martial; *pugnax, pugnacis* battle loving; *pugnare* to fight, go against; *pugna* hand fighting, boxing from Gr. *pyx, pugme (πύξ, πυγμή)* fist (philomachus, ruff, 160, 376) C. Linnaeus, 1758.

purpurascens L. somewhat purple coloured; *purpura* purple; *porphyra (πορφύρα)* a sea snail, the colouring substance from a number of sea snails of the genus *murex*, imperial dye, royal purple, deep red; (vidua, purple indigobird, 394, 1079) A. Reichenow, 1883.

purpurea/purpureus L. purple coloured; *purpura* purple; *porphyra (πορφύρα)* a sea snail, the colouring substance from a number of sea snails of the genus *murex*, imperial dye, royal purple, deep red; (ardea, purple heron, 62, 591, C. Linnaeus, 1766) (phoeniculus, green wood-hoopoe, 248, 162, J. F. Miller, 1784).

pusilla/pusillus L. very small; *pusillus* very small, short, tiny; diminutive of *pusus* little boy; the crake's common name is after Jean François Emmanuel *Baillon* (1744-1802), a French lawyer, collector and naturalist (merops, little bee-eater, 240, 187, P. L. S Müller, 1776) (pogoniulus, red-fronted tinkerbird, 254, 143, C. Dumont de Sainte Croix, 1816) (porzana, baillon's crake, 138, 327, P. S. Pallas, 1776).

pycnonotus Gr. thick-backed; *pycnos (πυκνός)* thick; *noton* or *notos* or *nota (νῶτον* or *νῶτος* or *νῶτα)* the back of humans and vertebrate animals (50).

pycnopygius Gr. dense-rumped; *pycnos (πυκνός)* thick; pyge *(πυγή)* rump (achaetops, rockrunner, 322, 780) P. Sclater, 1853.

pygargus Gr. white rump (Jobling); *pyge (πυγή)* backside, rump; *argos (ἀργός)* shiny, white; *pygargos (πύγαργος)* white-tailed eagle; Aeschylus compares Menelaus to the white-tailed eagle and Agamemnon to the golden eagle (circus, montagu's

harrier, 106, 504) C. Linnaeus, 1758.

pygoscelis Gr. legs at rump; *pyge (πυγή)* backside, rump; *skelos (σκέλος)* leg; *pygoscelis (πυγοσκελίς)* a waterbird mentioned by Hesychius, with its legs far to the back (44).

pyrenestes Gr. fruit-stone eater; *pyren pyrenos (πυρήν, πυρῆνος)* pip; *-estes (-εστης)* eater from verb *esthio (ἐσθίω)* to eat (58).

pytilia Gr. diminutive of *pitylus* grosbeak (58).

Q

quadrivirgata L. four streaked. *quadri-* four; *virga, ae* staff, green branch; *vireo* to be green, to be fresh, flourish; a reference to alternating dark and pale stripes on face (Roberts) (cercotrichas, bearded-scrub robin, 308, 937) A. Reichenow, 1879.

quartinia Roberts (2009) writes it means fourth in L. and that it was the fourth species of waxbill described by Bonaparte in *Conspectus Generum Avium,* and so does Jobling (1991, 197) but in 2010 (pp. 328) he mentions a French explorer in Abyssinia in 1839-1840 by the name R. *Quartin* Dillon! (coccopygia, yellow-bellied waxbill, 402, 1043) C. L. Bonaparte, 1851.

quelea probably from the English word *quail,* which has the alternative spelling *'qalia'* and *'qualea'* (Roberts, 2009) A suggestion by Jeffreys (at Jobling, 2010, pp. 328) is that the numbers of queleas are comparable to the quails *that fell upon the camp of Israelites;* (quelea, red-billed quelea, 388, 1025) C. Linnaeus, 1758.

querquedula L. it is a type of duck; possibly from *querquetulanus* of the forest or woodlands; *querquetum* or *quercetum* forest, woodland; *quercus* oak tree, spear, ship (anas, garganey, 84, 114) C. Linnaeus, 1758.

questi after exploring vessel *Quest;* the ship started off as a seal-hunting vessel and was used for the Shackleton-Rowett Antarctic expedition in 1920-1922; it sunk in 1962 (nesospiza, nightingale bunting, 414).

R

ralloides like a rail; L. *rallus* rail; Gr. *-oides* resembling; the common name comes from a local Italian word *sguacco,* quoted by Francis Willughby (1635-1672) (ardeola, squacco heron, 66, 594) G. A. Scopoli, 1769.

rallus L. rail; Fr. *rale;* Eng. *rail;* Dutch *ral;* Ger. *ralle;* L. *rallus* thin, light, rare (35).

ranivorus L. frog-eater; L. *rana,-ae* frog; Gr. *vora (βορά)* food, mostly of carnivore animals and from this word comes L. *vorare* to swallow, to devour (circus, african marsh-harrier, 106, 501) F. M. Daudin, 1800.

rapax L. rapacious; *rapax, -acis* grasping, rapacious, greedy, ravenous; *rapere* to seize, to tear, to snatch, to carry off (aquila, tawny eagle, 94, 529) C. J. Temminck, 1828.

recurvirostra L. recurved–billed; *recurvare* bend back, curve; *rostrum,-i* beak, bill; re + curvus (37).

regia L. regal; *regius,-a,-um* regal, of a king, royal, majestic; *rex, regis* king, dominant, protector; *regere* lead, direct, manage (vidua, shaft-tailed whydah, 392, 1074) C. Linnaeus, 1766.

regulorum L. of small kings, crowned; *regulus* petty king, prince, king of a small country; *rex, regis* king, dominant, protector; *regere* lead, direct, manage; *Regulus* is also the brightest star of the constellation of Leo and a Roman consul, captured by Carthaginians (balearica, crowned crane, 142, 307) E. T. Bennett, 1834.

regulus L. little king; *regulus* petty king, prince, king of a small country; *rex, regis* king, dominant, protector; *regere* lead, direct, manage; *Regulus* is also the brightest star of the constellation of Leo and a Roman consul, captured by Carthaginians (prodotiscus, brown-backed honeybird, 250, 127) C. J. Sundevall, 1850.

reichenowi/reichenovii after Anton *Reichenow* (1847-1941), a German ornithologist and expert on African birds despite the fact he had visited Africa only once in 1872 to 1873; he published Die Vogel Africas (the birds of Africa) from 1900 to 1905 (anthreptes, plain-backed sunbird, 374, 975, J. W. B. Gunning, 1909) (cryptospiza, red-faced crimsonwing, 400, 1046, G. Hartlaub, 1874).

repressa L. restrained; *reprimere* press back, prevent, check, restrain; re+premere (sterna, white-cheeked tern, 192, 465) E. Hartert, 1916.

retzii after Anders Jahan *Retzius* (1742-1821), a Swedish naturalist and Professor of Natural History or his son Anders Adolf Retzius (1796-1860) Professor of Anatomy at the Karolinska Institute or even his other son Carl Gustaf Retzius (1798-1833), a veterinary professor in Stockholm (Watkins & Beolens, 2003, pp. (prionops, retz's helmet-shrike, 364, 709) J. A. Wahlberg, 1856.

rhinopomastus Gr. covered nose; *ris, rinos* (ρίς, ρινός) nose; *poma, pomatos* (πῶμα, πώματος) lid, cover; *pomazo* (πωμάζω) to cover with a lid; *pomasteon* (πωμαστέον) covered with a lid; referring to covered nares (29).

rhinoptilus Gr. feathered nose; *ris, rinos (ρίς, ρινός)* nose; *ptilon (πτίλον)* feather (38).

rhodopareia Gr. red or rose cheeked; *rhodon (ρόδον)* rose; *pareia (παρειά)* cheek; the bird's common name commemorates James Sligo *Jameson* (1856-1888), an Irish hunter, explorer and naturalist who collected in South Africa among other places and died in the Congo of haemorrhagic fever; his *Story of the rear column of the Emin Pasha Relief Expedition* was published two years after his death (lagonosticta, jameson's firefinch, 402, 1064) T. von Heuglin, 1868.

ridibundus L. laughing; *ridibundus* laughing; *ridere* to laugh, ridicule (chroicocephalus, common black-headed gull, 186, 446 (larus) C. Linnaeus, 1799.

riparia L. frequenting a stream or river bank or bank-nesting; *ripa* river bank, shore (riparia, sand martin, 282, 744) C. Linnaeus, 1758

rissa Icelandic name *Rita* of the Black-legged kittiwake (Old Norse *Ryta*) (Jobling, 2010, pp. 336) (39).

robertsi after J. Austin *Roberts* (1883-1948), a zoologist and the most prominent ornithologist of the first half of the twentieth century in southern Africa; he worked at the Transvaal Museum for 36 years; although he had no formal academic training he received many academic awards, including an honorary doctorate; most memorable of course is his *Birds of South Africa*, first published in 1940 and a best seller since (Beolens & Watkins, 2003, pp. 288) (oreophilais, roberts's warbler, 338, 847) C. W. Benson, 1946.

robustus L. robust; *robustus* of oak, hard, robust, strong; *robur* oak, strength, vigor, force (poicephalus, cape parrot, 206, 221) J. F. Gmelin, 1788.

rochii after S. *Roch* (1829-1906) an army surgeon in Mauritius (cuculus, madagascar cuckoo, 212, 210) G. Hartlaub, 1862.

rogersi after Revd. Henry Martyn *Rogers* (1879-1926), resident chaplain on Tristan d'Acunha (Jobling, 2009, pp. 337) (inaccessible island rail, atlantisia, 414) P. Lowe, 1923.

roseicolis L. rosy necked; *roseus* rosy; *collis* necked, *collum* neck (agapornis, rosy-faced lovebird, 208, 227) L. J. P. Vieillot, 1817.

roseus L. rosy, rosy coloured; *roseus* rosy, red; (phoenicopterus, greater flamingo, 74, 605 (ruber=red) C. Linnaeus, 1758) (sturnus or pastor, rose-coloured starling, 370, C. Linnaeus, 1758).

rossae after Lady Ann *Ross* (died 1857), wife of Rear-Admiral Sir James Clark Ross (1802-1862), Arctic and Antarctic explorer, who has a gull, an island and a sea named after him; Gould described this species based on a drawing by Lieut JR Stack, and from feathers shed from the wings and tail of a bird kept by Lady Ross at St Helena (Roberts, 2009) (musophaga, ross's turaco, 210, 247) J. Gould, 1851-2

rostratula L. small-beaked; *rostrum* bill; diminutive of *rostratus* beaked, curved; its bill is smaller than the true snipes (36).

rowettia after John Quiller *Rowett* (1876-1924) English businessman and sponsor of Shackleton-Rowett expedition to the Antarctic 1921-1922 (Jobling, 2010, pp. 338) (414).

ruber L. red; *rubere* to be red, to blush (greater flamingo, phoenicopterus, 74, 605) C. Linnaeus, 1758.

rubetra L. red, reddish; *ruber,-ri* red; *rubere* to be red, to blush (saxicola, whinchat, 304, 945) C. Linnaeus, 1758.

rubiginosus L. rusty coloured; *robiginosus* or *rubiginosus* rusty; *rubigo* or *robigo* rust, mould (ploceus, chestnut weaver, 384, 1019) E. Rüpell, 1840.

rubricata L. red; *rubricata* red, painted red with ochre; *rubrica* red earth, red ocher, a law with its title written in red (lagonosticta, african for blue-billed firefinch, 402, 1063) M. H. C. Lichtenstein, 1823.

rubricauda L. red-tailed; *ruber,-ri* red; *rubere* to be red, to blush; *cauda* tail (phaethon, red-tailed tropicbird, 50, 564) P. Boddaert, 1783.

ruddi after Charles Dunnel *Rudd* (1844-1916), an English businessman in South Africa; the main business associate of Cecil John Rhodes, Chairman of De Beers Mining Company and sponsor of expeditions in tropical Africa, including C. H.

B. Grant (apalis, rudd's apalis, 326, 853, C. H. B. Grant, 1908) (heteromirafra, rudd's lark, 370, 867, C. H. B. Grant, 1908)

rudis L. according to Jobling *rudis* means wild or rude; according to Roberts it means foil; we found it means raw, rude, rough, coarse, wild and also foil, sword, practice sword of gladiators; *rudere* bellow, roar, bray, creak loudly (ceryle, pied kingfisher, 234, 184) C. Linnaeus, 1758.

rueppellii after Wilhelm Peter Eduard Simon *Rüppel* (1794-1884), a German collector; he explored northern and eastern Africa in two expeditions; he wrote *Reisen in Nubien, Kordofan und dem Petraischen Arabien* and *Systematische Ubersicht der Vogel Nordost-Afrikas* (eupodotis, rüppels korhaan, 148, 300, J. A. Wahlberg, 1856) (gyps, rüppels vulture, 86, 489, A. E. Brehm, 1852) (poicephalus, rüppels parrot, 206, 226, J. E. Gray, 1848)

rufa/rufus L. red, ruddy, rufous; *rufus,-a, um* red, yellow-red; *'in ornithology rufus, rufa and rufum cover a wide spectrum of colours from yellow, orange and brown to crimson, scarlet and*

purple' (Jobling, 2010, pp. 341) (anhinga, african darter, 56, 570 F. M. Daudin, 1802) (cursorius, Burchell's courser, 180, 424, J. Gould, 1837) (sarothrura, red-chested flufftail, 140, 317, L. J. P Vieillot, 1819).

rufescens L. reddish; *rufus* red, ruddy, rufous; (acrocephalus, greater swamp-warbler, 320, 802, R. B. Sharpe & A. Bouvier, 1876) (pelecanus, pink-backed pelican, 58, 615, J. F. Gmelin, 1789) (sylvietta, long-billed crombec, 328, 785, L. J. P Vieillot, 1817)

ruficapilla L. red-capped; *rufus* red, ruddy, rufous; *capilla* cape, cloak, cassock; *capillus* hair, hair of head (phylloscopus, yellow-throated woodland-warbler, 314, 806, J. C. Sundevall, 1850) (sylvietta, red-capped crombec, 328, 784, J. V. Barbosa du Bocage, 1877).

ruficauda L. red-tailed; *rufus* red, ruddy, rufous; *cauda* tail (cichladusa, rufous-tailed palm-thrush, 312, 936) G. Hartlaub, 1857.

ruficollis L. red-necked; *rufus* red, ruddy, rufous; *collum* neck, throat (calidris, red-necked stint, 164, 367, P. S. Pallas, 1776) (jynx,

red-throated wryneck, 256, 129, J. G. Wagler, 1830) (tachybaptus, little grebe, 60, 560, P. S. Pallas, 1764).

ruficrista L. red-crested; *rufus* red, ruddy, rufous; *crista, -ae* crest, plume, helmet (lophotis, red-crested korhaan, 146, 296) A. Smith, 1836.

rufigena L. & Gr. red-cheeked. L. *rufus* red, ruddy, rufous; Gr. *genys, genyos (γένυς, γένυος)* cheek, jaw (caprimulgus, rufous-cheeked nightjar, 224, 271) A. Smith, 1845.

rufilatus L. red-flanked; *rufus* red, ruddy, rufous; *latus* side, flank (cisticola, tinkling cisticola, 332, 828) G. Hartlaub, 1870.

rufinus L. golden, golden-red, red; *rufus* red. ruddy, rufous; (buteo, long-legged buzzard, 102, 524) P. J. Cretzschmar, 1829.

rufiventris L. red bellied; *rufus* red, ruddy, rufous; *venter, ventris* belly, abdomen; Eng. *ventri*loquist (accipiter, rufous chested or red breasted sparrowhawk, 108, 519, Dr Sir Andrew Smith, 1830) (ardeola, rufous-bellied heron, 66, 595, C. J. Sundevall, 1850) (parus,

rufous-bellied tit, 290, 740, J. V. Barboza du Bocage, 1877).

rufocinnamomea L. red cinnamon; *rufus* red, ruddy, rufous; *cinnamomum* cinnamon (mirafra, flappet lark, 264, 863) T. Salvadori, 1865.

rufofuscus L. dark or dusky red; *rufus* red, ruddy, rufous; *fuscus* brown, dusky, dark, swarthy (buteo, jackal buzzard, 104, 526) J. R. Forster, 1798.

rupestris L. rock-dwelling, living among rocks; *rupes, rupis* rock, cliff (monticola, cape rock-thrush, 300, 897) L. J. P Vieillot, 1818.

rupicoloides L. & Gr. like rupicolus (rock kestrel); *rupes, rupis* rock, cliff; *colere* live in, inhabit; Gr. *-oides* resembling; the common name *kestrel* from French *crècerelle*, derives from *crécelle* ratchet, noisemaker (falco, greater kestrel, 122, 547) A. Smith, 1829.

rupicolus L. rock-dwelling; *rupes, rupis* rock, cliff; *colere* live in, inhabit; (falco, rock kestrel, 122, 546) F. M. Daudin, 1800.

rustica L. of the country, rural, rustic, homely, plain, simple; *rus, ruris* country, farm; Eng. *rural* (hirundo, barn swallow, 278, 748) C. Linnaeus, 1758.

rynchops Gr. Roberts (2009) supports bill face, referring to strange bills; *rynchos (ρύγχος) bill, beak, snout; ops (ὤψ)* eye, face; Jobling (2010, pp. 344) agrees with the first part but says the second part comes from Gr. *kopto (κόπτω)* to cut off; *'the upper mandible being as if cut'* (38).

S

sabini after General Sir Edward <u>Sabine</u> (1788-1883), a British army officer, astronomer, physicist and explorer; he was a Fellow, a Treasurer and eventually President of the Royal Society; the gull was found by his brother Joseph, who named it after him, on the expedition in search of the Northwest Passage in 1818; Sir Edward was the expedition's astronomer and geologist (xema, sabine's gull, 186) J. Sabine, 1819.

sabota Tswana; *sebotha* or *sibutha* or *sebothe* is the name for various species of lark (calendulauda, sabota lark, 266, 868) A. Smith, 1836.

sagittarius L. archer; *sagittarius* archer; *sagitta* arrow Jobling (2009, pp. 345) reports that Vosmaer (1804) thought this bird moved like an *advancing crossbowman,* so it was given the name *'Sagittaire'* which means archer; another suggestion is that the crest on its head looks like a quiver of arrows; a third explanation is that it is the last constellation of the Zodiac, *Sagittarius* and *Serpentarius* is the next constellation now known by its Gr. name, Ophiuchus, and thought by some to be the 13th constellation of the Zodiac since his leg crosses the Zodiac; the corruption of the word *Sagittaire* gave the bird its common name 'Secretaire' for secretary; another popular explanation is that the name derives from the crest of feathers that make it look like a secretary with quill pens behind its ears; a third one, and the one we like the most is that it is the corruption of the Arabic name of the bird طائر صياد *sagr-et-tair meaning hunter-bird* (40).

salpornis Gr. war-trumpeter bird, trumpeter; *salpinktes (σαλπιγγτής)* trumpeter; *salpizo (σαλπίζω)* to trumpet, to toot; *salpinx (σάλπιγξ)* trumpet; *ornis ornithos (ὄρνις, ὄρνιθος)* bird in ancient Gr.; the word for bird was both male and female in ancient Gr.; in modern Gr. it is female and it means chicken (53).

salvini after Osbert *Salvin* (1835-1898), an English naturalist, ornithologist and Curator of ornithology at Cambridge University; he co-authored with Frederick Godman the 40-volume *Biologia Centrali Americana* in 1879, an almost complete catalogue of Middle American species; he has also written *Exotic Ornithology* and *Nomenclatur Avium Neotropicum;* his and Godman's names were given to the prestigious Medal of the British Ornithologists' Union (pachyptila, salvin's prion, 34, 664, G. Mathews, 1912) (thalassarche, salvin's albatross, 24, 647, L. W. Rothchild, 1893).

sandvicencis the name *sandvicencis* usually means that the species was found in Hawaii, but this bird is not found there; James Cook named Hawaii the Sandwich islands, to comemmorate his sponsor John Montag, 4th Earl of Sandwich; the name of this bird probably refers to Sandwich, Kent, Latham's type locality; sandwich is Old English or Scandinavian and it means 'a trading center on sand'

from 'wik' or 'vik' that means settlement (sterna, sandwich tern, 190, 455) J. Latham, 1787.

sanfordi after L. Cutler ˙*Sanford* (1868-1950)(Leland, Leyland or Leonard?? the first being the strongest candidate), an American zoologist; he co-authored *The Waterfowl family;* he was a trustee of the American Museum of Natural History, organiser of the Whitney-Sanford South Pacific expeditions and sponsor of the AMNH Mt Hagen Expedition; many scientific names of different species of animals, from dinosaurs to butterflies include *sanfordi* (diomedea, northern royal albatross, 22, 644) R. C Murphy, 1917.

sarkidiornis Gr. flesh and bird; *sarkidion (σαρκίδιον)* small flesh, proud flesh (another name for granulation tissue); *sarx, sarkos (σάρξ, σαρκός)* flesh; *ornis ornithos (ὄρνις, ὄρνιθος)* bird in ancient Gr.; the word for bird was both male and female in ancient Gr.; in modern Gr. it is female and it means chicken; it used to mean the front muscle of the thigh and all the muscles in plural; Eng. sarcasm (27).

sarothrura a broom or brush-shaped tail; *sarothron*

(σάρωθρον) broom; *oura (οὐρά)* tail (35).

saxicola L. stone dweller; *saxum* stone, big rock, cliff, stone wall; *cola* inhabitant; *colere* to dwell, inhabit, live in (54).

schalowi after Hermann *Schalow* (1852-1925), a German banker and amateur ornithologist; he worked with *Cabanis* and *Reichenow;* his writings include *Die Musophagidae* and *Beitrage zur Vogelfauna der Mark Brandenburg;* the Berlin National History Museum library is named after him too (tauraco, schalow's turaco, 210, 244) A. Reichenow, 1891.

schlegelli after Hermann *Schlegel* (1804-1884), a German zoologist, who was the first one to use three names (trinomials) to describe separate races; he was Director of the Rijksmuseum van Natuurlijke Historie in Leiden; his writings include *Fauna Japonica-Aves* and *Kritische Ubersicht der Europaischen Vogel* (cercomela, karoo chat, 302, 953) J. A. Wahlberg, 1855.

schoenicola Gr. & L. to inhabit rushes or reeds; Gr. *schoenos (σχοῖνος)* reed, rush; L. *cola* inhabitant; *colere* to dwell, inhabit, live in (51).

schoenobaenus Gr. to go to reed, reed-dwelling; schoenos *(σχοῖνος)* reed, rush; veno *(βαίνω)* to go (acrocephalus, sedge warbler, 318, 795). C. Linnaeus, 1758.

schoutedenapus after Henri Eugéne Alphonse Hubert *Schouteden* (1881-1972), a Belgian zoologist who travelled extensively in the Congo; his area of expertise were swifts but wrote on entomology as well; he wrote *De Vogels van Belgisch-Congo en van Ruanda-Urundi.* Gr. *apus (ἄπους)* legless, without feet or legs; privative α- without; *pous, podos (ποῦς, ποδός)* foot (32).

scirpaceus L. *scirpus* reed, bulrush or sedge; *–aceus* resembling or having the nature of (acrocephalus, eurasian reed-warbler, 318, 796) J. Hermann, 1804.

scita L. pretty, neat, fine; *scitus* neat, nice, excellent; *sciscere* to approve by voting, investigate, inquire (stenostira, fairy flycatcher, 328, 778) L. J. P. Vieillot, 1818.

sclateri after William Lutley *Sclater* (1863-1944), an English ornithologist and museum director; he was the son of Philip

Lutley Sclater and president of the British Ornithologist's Union, Deputy-Superintendent of the Indian Museum in Calcutta, Director of the South African Museum, in Cape Town, president of the South African Ornithologist's Union and editor of the *Ibis;* after South Africa he worked for 30 years at the Natural History British Museum; he was killed by a V1 flying bomb in London; he wrote *Systema Avium Aethiopicarum, Flora and Fauna of South Africa* and also completed works started by others such as *The Birds of South Africa, Birds of Africa* and *The Birds of Kenya Colony and the Uganda Protectorate* (spizocorys, sclater's lark, 270, 894) G. E. Shelley, 1902.

scleroptila Gr. stiff feathers; *skleros (σκληρός)* hard, tough, stiff; *ptilon (πτίλον)* feather, plume (26).

scopifrons L. with a brush on the forehead; *scopa* broom, brush; *scopare* to brush, sweep away; *frons frontis* forehead, brow, face, front, forepart of anything (prionops, chestnut-fronted helmet-shrike, 364, 710) W. Peters, 1854.

scopus either brush or broom from L. *scopa* or watcher, guard from Gr. *skopos (σκοπός)* guard, watcher, purpose, aim, focus;

Gr. skia *(σκιά)* shadow or shade sounds highly unlikely (43).

scotopelia Gr. dark pigeon; *skotos (σκότος) (skotadi σκοτάδι* in modern Gr.) darkness; *peleia (πέλεια)* the wild pigeon *columba oenas* thus named because of its dark colour; *peleiai (πέλειαι)* priestesses that could foresee the future as did the magic pigeons of Dodoni; *pelios (πελιός)* bruised; *Pelias*, king of Iolkos, was named after the dark mark he had on his face, by a horse kick when he was deserted with his twin brother, *Neleas*, by their mother (33).

scotops Gr. dark face or eye; *skotos (σκότος) (skotadi σκοτάδι* in modern Gr.) darkness; *ops (ὤψ, ὀπός)* face (crithagra, forest canary, 408, 1123, C. J. Sundevall, 1850) (eremomela, green-capped eremomela, 324, 788, C. J. Sundevall, 1850)

scriptoricauda L. writing tail or as Roberts claims written tail referring to obscure tail barring; *scriptorius* writing; *scribere* to write; *cauda* tail (campethera, speckle-throated woodpecker, 258, 131,) A. Reichenow, 1896.

semipalmatus L. half or small palmate; *semi* half; *palma,-ae* palm, palm-tree; (limnodromus, asiatic dowitcher, 168, 1141) E. Blyth, 1848.

semirufa L. half rufous; *semi* half; *rufa* red, yellow-red, ruddy, rufous; (hirundo, red-breasted swallow, 274, 757) C. J. Sundevall, 1850.

semitorquata/semitorquatus L. half-collared; *semi* half; *torquata* wearing a neck chain; *torques* or *torcues* necklace, crown; *torquere* turn, twist, torture, torment, distort (alcedo, half-collared kingfisher, 234, 173, W. J. Swainson, 1923) (certhilauda, eastern long-billed lark, 262, 881, A. Smith, 1836) (polihierax, pygmy falcon, 114, 544, A. Smith, 1836) (streptopelia, red-eyed dove, 202, 286, E. Rüppell, 1837).

senegala/senegalensis/ senegallus/senegalus from Senegal; *Senegal* is the westernmost country of Africa and takes its name from the *Sénégal River;* the derivation of the name of the river is disputed; one popular version is that it is from the *Wolof* phrase *sunu gaal* 'our canoe', believed to be the wrong answer Portuguese traders got when they asked the name of the river; another version is that it derives from

the Berber *Zenaga* people and another from the medieval town of *Shangana* described by a traveller by the name al-Bakri; another one proposed by the Serer people is that it comes from the combination of the name of one of their deities *Sene* and the word *O Gal* 'body of water' (centropus, senegal coucal, 218, 218, C. Linnaeus, 1766) (chalcomitra, scarlet-chested sunbird, 378, 982, C. Linnaeus, 1766) (ephippiorhynchus, saddle-billed stork, 72, 625, G. Ghaw, 1800) (eupodotis, white-bellied korhaan, 148, 304, L. J. P. Vieillot, 1820) (halcyon, woodland kingfisher, 236, 178, C. Linnaeus, 1766) (hirundo, mosque swallow, 274, 759, C. Linnaeus, 1766) (lagonosticta, red-billed firefinch, 402, 1061, C. Linnaeus, 1766) (otus, african scops-owl, 220, 253, W. J. Swainson, 1837) (podica, african finfoot, 134, 314, L. J. P. Vieillot, 1817) (streptopelia, laughing dove, 202, 281, C. Linnaeus, 1766) (tchagra, black-crowned tchagra, 360, 692, C. Linnaeus, 1766) (vanellus, african wattled lapwing, 158, 412, C. Linnaeus, 1766) (zosterops, african yellow white-eye, 344, 821, C. L. Bonaparte, 1850).

senegaloides resembling Senegal; *Senegal* is the

westernmost country of Africa and takes its name from the *Sénégal River* (see above)*;* Gr. *-oides* resembling (halcyon, mangrove kingfisher, 236, 179) A. Smith, 1834.

sephaena uncertain; probably from Tswana; Jobling (2010, pp. 354) suggests there is a relation with *paena* (pp. 288) the name *Phena* or *Phene* for the Kalahari scrub robin (dendroperdix, crested francolin, 128, 63) A. Smith, 1836.

serinus suggested from French *Serin* canary and Jobling (2010, pp. 354) takes it further to suggest that it is a corruption from L. *citrinus* citron-coloured, yellow; our suggestion would be from Gr. *Serin* (Σειρήν) and in the plural *Sirenes* (Σειρῆνες) the winged mythological creatures that tried to attract Ulysses with their enchanting song (!) and a small singing bird mentioned by Hesychios (59).

serpentarius L. hunter of reptiles; *serpens, serpentis* snake, dragon, a crawler; the name implies the bird's preference of hunting serpents or the constellation of *Serpentarius* now known by its Gr. name *Ophiuchus*, considered by some

as the 13th constellation of the Zodiac, since his leg crosses the Zodiac and that *Sagittarius* is the 12th constellation of the Zodiac (sagittarius, secretarybird, 142, 542) J. F. Miller, 1779.

serrator L. jagged, serrated, notched, sawyer; *serra* saw (morus, australian gannet, 52, 568) G. R. Gray, 1843.

shelleyi after Captain George Ernest *Shelley* (1840-1910), a geologist and ornithologist and the great poet's (Percy Bysshe Shelley) nephew; he retired with the rank of captain from the Grenadier Guards; he wrote on the birds of Egypt and *A Monograph of the Cinnyridae, or Family of Sunbirds* and *The Birds of Africa* (cinnyris, shelley's sunbird, 378, 997, B. Alexander, 1899) (scleroptila, shelley's francolin, 130, 66, W. R. Ogilvie-Grant, 1891).

sheppardia after Peter A. *Sheppard* (1875-1958), a British farmer, zoologist, collector and settler in Rhodesia (now Zimbabwe) and Mozambique (54).

sigelus Gr. silent; *sigelos* or *sigalos* (σιγηλός or σιγαλός) silent, still, shy, slow-moving;

sige (σιγή) silence, absence of noise (54).

signata L. marked, distinctive, distinct, well marked; *signare* to mark, to stamp, to print, to designate; *signum* mark, sign, token, design (cercotrichas, brown scrub-robin, 308, 938) C. J. Sundevall, 1850.

silens L. silent; *silens, silentis* silent, still; *silentium* silence; *silere* to be silent, calm down, be quiet (sigelus, fiscal flycatcher, 340, 917) G. Shaw, 1809.

similis L. similar to, resembling; *similis* like, similar; *presumably referring to its similarity to many other large pipits* (Roberts, 2009) (anthus, long-billed pipit, 350, 1108) T. C. Jerdon, 1840.

simplex L. simple, plain; *simplex, simplicis* single, simple, natural, straightforward, frank, sincere, naive (pogoniulus, green tinkerbird, 254, 141) Fischer & A. Reichenow, 1884.

sinuata L. curved; *sinuatus* bend into a curve; *sinus* curve, fold; *sinus* curve, bending; *sinuare* to wind, to curve, to bend (cercomela, sickle-winged chat, 302, 952) C. J. Sundevall, 1858.

smithi/smithii after Sir Andrew *Smith* (1797-1872), first Director of the South African Museum, Cape Town; he was a Scottish surgeon, explorer, ethnologist and zoologist; he wrote *Illustrations of the Zoology of South Africa* and is thus considered the father of South African Zoology; travelling through South Africa he collected and described many species; he was sent among the various people of the region on secret missions and met historical figures such as Dingaan, Mzilikazi and even Charles Darwin; he also wrote about the Xsosa, the Bushmen and other peoples of southern Africa (anas, cape shoveller, 82, 108, E. Hartert, 1891) (turdus, karoo thrush, 298, 908, C. L. Bonaparte, 1850).

smithii after Christen *Smith* (1785-1816), *Norwegian botanist and zoologist who died on Tuckey's ill-fated Congo epedition* (Jobling, 2010, pp. 358) (hirundo, wire tailed swallow, 278, 751) W. E. Leach, 1818.

smithornis after Sir Andrew *Smith* (1797-1872), first Director of the South African Museum, Cape Town (see smithi/smithii);

ornis ornithos (ὄρνις ὄρνιθος) bird in ancient Gr. (47).

socius L. sociable; *socius* associated, allied, friend, companion, partner, ally (philetairus, sociable weaver, 382, 1007) J. Latham, 1790.

solitarius L. solitary; *solitarius* solitary, lonely; *solus* only, lonely, single, deserted (cuculus, red-chested cuckoo, 212, 205) J. F. Stephens, 1815.

soror L. sister; *soror, sororis* sister, friend, similar, prostitute; *this being a sister species to B. molitor*; Eng. sorority (Roberts, 2009)(batis, pale batis, 346, 717) A. Reichenow, 1903.

souzae after Jose Augusto de *Sousa* (1837-1889), a Portuguese ornithologist, Director of Ornithology at the Museum of Lisbon; although he never visited Africa, he wrote many articles on its birds (Beolens & Watkins, 2003, pp. 318) (lanius, Souza's shrike, 358, 726) J. V. Barboza du Bocage, 1878.

sparsa L. scattered or speckled, depending weather the name refers to the scattered white spots or the distribution of the bird; *sparsus* freckled; *spargere* to strew, scatter, sprinkle, spot; from Gr. *spargao* (σπαργάω) to be full (anas, african black duck, 82, 103) T.C. Eyton, 1838.

spatulatus L. spatulate, having a broad, rounded end; *spathula* or *spatula* sword, back; *spatha* broad sword; *spatium* space, place, width; *spatiosus* wide, spacious, long (coracias, racket-tailed roller, 242, 170,) R. Trimen, 1880.

spermestes Gr. seed eater; *sperma* (σπέρμα) seed; *-estes* (-εστης) eater from verb *esthio* (ἐσθίω) to eat (58).

spheniscus Gr. little wedge; *sphen, sphenos* (σφήν, σφηνός) wedge; refers either to the wings of the bird that *provide powerful propulsion* (Jobling, 2010, pp. 361) or the shape of the whole bird (*streamlined swimming body*) (Roberts, 2009) (44).

sphenoeacus Gr. wedge-like helm; *sphen, sphenos* (σφήν, σφηνός) wedge; *oiax, oiakos* (οἴαξ, οἴακος) helm, metaphorically the helm of government; *refers to the wedge-shaped retrices* (Roberts, 2009) (51).

spilodera Gr. spotted neck; *spilos (σπίλος)* spot, stigma, smudge, blemish; *deros* or *deras (δέρος or δέρας)* skin (hirundo, south african cliff-swallow, 276, 760) C. J. Sundevall, 1850.

spilogaster Gr. spotted belly, underparts; *spilos (σπίλος)* spot, stigma, smudge, blemish; *gaster, gasteros (γαστήρ, γαστέρος)* belly; Eng. *gastr*ic, *gastr*itis, *gastr*onomy (aquila, african hawk-eagle, 98, 533) C. L. Bonaparte, 1850.

spilonotos Gr. spotted back; *spilos (σπίλος)* spot, stigma, smudge, blemish; *noton* or *notos* or *nota (νῶτον or νῶτος or νῶτα)* the back of humans and vertebrate animals (salpornis, spotted creeper, 258, 896) J. Franklin, 1831.

spinosus L. thorny, prickly: *referring to carpal spurs* (Roberts, 2009); *spina* thorn, prickle, fishbone, spine (vanellus, spur-winged lapwing, 156, 410) C. Linnaeus, 1758.

spizocorys Gr. finch lark; *spiza (σπίζα)* finch; *korys, korythos (κόρυς, κόρυθος)* helmet made of copper, casque, lark; *corysso (κορύσσω)* to put on a helmet (53).

splendens L. shining; *splendens* shining, gleaming, glittering; *splendere* to shine, to be brilliant, illustrious, bright, radiant (corvus, house crow, 288, 721) L. J. P. Vieillot, 1817.

sporaeginthus Gr. seed waxbill or seed finch; *sporos σπόρος* seed; *aeginthos* or *aegithos (αἴγινθος or αἴγιθος)* probably the common sparrow; waxbill genus according to Roberts, probably a finch according to Jobling (2010, pp. 363) (57).

sporopipes Gr. looking for seeds; *sporos σπόρος* seed; *opipevo* or *opiptevo (ὀπιπεύω* or *ὀπιπτεύω)* to watch, to stare at, to ambush (56).

spreo French *spréo* or L. meaning starling; *spreuw* in Afrikaans (55).

squamifrons L. scaly forehead; *squameus* scaly; *squama* scale; *frons* forehead, brow, fron, facade, exterior, appearance, look (sporopipes, scaly-feathered finch, 404, 1005) A. Smith, 1836.

squatarola from *sgatarola*, a Venetian name for a plover (pluvialis, grey plover, 160, 395) C. Linnaeus, 1758.

stactolaema Gr. with drip like marks on throat or ash-coloured throat; *staktos (στακτός)* driping, trickling; *laemos (λαιμός)* throat; *stakte* or *stahte (στάκτη* or *στάχτη)* ash, the colour of ash; *staktes* or *stahtes (στακτής* or *σταχτής)* ashy, ashen, ash-coloured (28).

stagnatilis L. of pools or marshes; *stagnum* standing water, pool, swamp, slow river (tringa, marsh sandpiper, 168, 353) J. M. Bechstein, 1803.

starki after Arthur Cowell *Stark* (1846 -1899), a British physician, naturalist and collector, who was killed at the siege of Ladysmith during the Anglo-Boer war (Jobling, 2010, pp. 364) author of Vols 1 and 2 of *Birds of South Africa* (Roberts, 2009, pp. 891) and co-author, with W. L. Sclater of *Fauna of South Africa* (Beolens & Watkins, 2003, pp. 321) (spizocorys, stark's lark, 270, 891) G. E. Shelley, 1902.

steganopus Gr. web-footed; *stegane (στεγάνη)* covering; *steganos (στεγανός)* covering to prohibit humidity, water proof; *pus, podos (πούς, ποδός)* foot (36).

stellaris L. starred, starry or speckled; *stella* star (botaurus, eurasian bittern, 68, 602) C. Linnaeus, 1758.

stellata L. set with stars, starred, starry or speckled, *referring to white supraloral and throat spots* (Roberts, 2009) *stella* star (pogonocichla, white-starred robin, 312, 924) L. J. P. Vieillot, 1818.

stenostira Gr. narrow tail; *stenos στενός* narrow, thin; *steira (στείρα)* ship's beak, forepart of keel (50).

stephanoaetus Gr. crowned eagle; *stephanos (στέφανος)* wreath; *stefo (στέφω)* to crown; *aetos (ἀετός)* eagle, king of birds (40).

stercorarius L. living or feeding on dung; from the bird's habit to pursue other birds until they dropped their food, once thought to be excrement; *stercoreus* filthy; *stercorare* to manure; *stercus* dung (38).

sterna old English names *stern*, *stearn* or *starn* for the Black Tern (Jobling, 2010, pp. 365) (39).

stierlingi after Dr N. *Stierling*, a German naturalist and taveller who collected in Malawi (then Nyasaland) and Tanzania (then Tanganyika) from 1887 to 1901 (Beolens & Watkins, 2003, pp. 324) (calamonastes, stierling's wren-warbler, 322, 859) A. Reichenow, 1901.

stolidus L. stupid or dull; *stolidus* fool, dull, stupid, insensible, inert; like anous, because they were tame and rather easy to catch (anous, brown noddy, 196, 472) C. Linnaeus, 1758.

streptopelia Gr. collared dove; *streptos (στρεπτός)* neck-chain made of twisted metal or chain, collar; *strefo (στρέφω)* to turn, to twist; *peleia (πέλεια)* the wild pigeon *Columba oenas* thus named because of its dark colour; *peleiai (πέλειαι)* priestesses that could foresee the future as did the magic pigeons of Dodoni; *pelios (πελιός)* bruised; *Pelias*, king of Iolkos, was named after the dark mark he had on his face, by a horse kick when he was deserted with his twin brother, *Neleas*, by their mother (34).

striata/striatus L. striated, striped, streaked; *striare* to striate, provide with channels, wrinkle; *stria* furrow (butorides, green-backed heron, 68, 596, C.

Linnaeus, 1758) (colius, speckled mousebird, 232, 197, J. F. Gmelin, 1789) (muscicapa, spotted flycatcher, 340, 919, P. S. Pallas, 1764)

strix Gr. owl, screech-owl; *strix, strigos (στρίξ, στριγός)* a night bird thus called for its screechy voice; L. *strix, strigis* screech-owl (bird of bad omen), vampire, evil spirit (sucks children's blood); *striga* ghost (33).

struthio Gr. sparrow; *struthion (στρουθίον)* diminutive of *struthos (στρουθός)* sparrow; in a number of languages there is the root *trozdo-* that gave us words that mean different bird names such as Lithuanian *strazdas*, Russian дрозд, English thrush, Ancient English *throstle*, Irish truid, Latin *turdus* etc (26).

sturmii after Johann Heinrich Christian Friedrich <u>Sturm</u> (1805-1862), a German bird artist and collector (Jobling, 2010, pp. 368) (ixobrychus, dwarf bittern, 68, 601) J. G. Wagler, 1827.

sturnus L. starling; *sturnus, -i* starling; Gr. *astralos (ἀστραλός)* starling according to Hesychius (55).

subaureus L. gold underneath or pale gold; *sub-* underneath, near to, close to, somewhat; *aureus* golden, ornamented with gold; *aurum* gold (ploceus, yellow weaver, 382, 1014) A. Smith, 1839.

subbuteo L. related to a buzzard; *sub-* underneath, near to, close to, somewhat; *buteo* species of hawk, buzzard (falco, eurasian hobby, 118, 554) C. Linnaeus, 1758.

subcaeruleum L. pale blue, nearly blue; *sub-* underneath, near to, close to, somewhat; *caeruleum* blue (parisoma, chestnut-vented tit-babbler, 328, 817) L. J. P. Vieillot, 1817.

subcinnamomea L. cinnamon-coloured underneath; *sub-* underneath, near to, close to, somewhat; *cinnamomeus* c i n n a m o n - c o l o u r e d; *cinnamomum* cinnamon; Gr. *kinnamomon* (κιννάμωμον); according to Herodot the word comes from Hebrew; (euryptila, cinnamon-breasted warbler, 322, 860) A. Smith, 1847.

subcoronata L. somewhat crowned or beneath the crown; if it means beneath the crown then it probably refers to the pale

supercilium; *sub-* underneath, near to, close to, somewhat; *coronare* to crown; *corona* crown Gr. *korone* (κορώνη) crown (certhilauda, karoo long-billed lark, 262, 882) A. Smith, 1843.

subflava/subflavus L. yellow below; *sub-* underneath, near to, close to, somewhat; *flavus* yellow, gold, blonde, flaxen; (prinia, tawy-flanked prinia, 338, 842, J. F. Gmelin, 1789) (sporaeginthus, orange-breasted waxbill, 398, 1039, L. J. P. Vieillot, 1819).

subminuta L. less than or somewhat small; it is compared to the larger *little stint*; *sub-* underneath, near to, close to, somewhat; *minuta* small; *minuere* to make smaller; Jobling (2010, pp. 371) writes it means it is near to *tringa minuta* (calidris, long-toed stint, 164, 369) A. von Mittendorf, 1853.

subruficapilla L. almost red-haired or near to Neddicky (fulvicapilla); *sub-* underneath, near to, close to, somewhat; *rufus* red, ruddy, rufous; *capillus* hair (of head or beard) (cisticola, grey-backed cisticola, 332, 829) A. Smith, 1843.

subruficollis L. reddish-necked; *sub-* underneath, near to, close to, somewhat; *rufus* red, ruddy, rufous; *collum* neck (trygnites, buff-breasted sandpiper, 160, 374) L. J. P. Vieillot, 1819.

substriata L. striped underneath; *sub-* underneath, near to, close to, somewhat; *striare* to striate, provide with channels, wrinkle; *stria* furrow (phragmacia, namaqua warbler, 338, 846) A. Smith, 1842.

sula Norwegian name for a gannet (Jobling, 2010, pp. 373) Icelandic foolish person, Gaelic sharp-sighted, Gr. to rob or plunder (Roberts) (sula, red-footed booby, 52, 568) C. Linnaeus, 1766.

sulphurata/us L. sulphur-coloured; *sulfur* sulphur, thunder; sulphur is a chemical element with atomic number 16 and symbol S, abundant in nature and has a bright yellow colour (crithagra, brimstone canary, 406, 1125) C. Linnaeus, 1766.

sulphureopectus L. yellow-breasted; *sulfur* sulphur, thunder; sulphur is a chemical element with atomic number 16 and symbol S, abundant in nature and has a bright yellow colour; *pectus, pectoris* breast, heart, soul(telophorus, orange-breasted bush-shrike, 362, 701) R. Lesson, 1831.

sumatrana from Sumatra; *Sumatra* is the sixth largest island in the world and is part of Indonesia in the Indian ocean; the island has lost 50% of its tropical rainforest in 35 years and a lot of species are critically endangered; Sumatra was known as the island of gold or land of gold; the indigenous people had no name for the island (sterna, black-naped tern, 194, 458) S. Raffles, 1822.

superciliaris L. with an eyebrow; *supercilium* eyebrow, pride, arrogance; *super + cilium* over, above + upper eyelid (petronia, yellow-throated petronia, 380, 1088) E. Blyth, 1845.

superciliosus L. eyebrowed; *superciliosus* arrogant, strict, sad faced, serious; *supercilium* eyebrow, pride, arrogance; *super + cilium* over, above + upper eyelid (centropus, white-browed coucal, 218, 219, W. Hemprich & Ehrenberg, 1833) (merops, Madagascar bee-eater, 238, 192, C. Linnaeus, 1766).

swainsonii after William John *Swainson* (1789-1855), a

naturalist and bird illustrator among other things; he travelled to Brazil and New Zealand, collected and wrote *Birds of Brazil* and the bird section of Sir John Richardson's *Fauna Boreali-Americana;* he contributed to Lardner's *Cabinet Encyclopedia* and Jardine's *Naturalist's Library* (pternistis, swainson'a spurfowl, 126, 74) A. Smith, 1836.

swynnertonia/swynnertoni after Charles Francis Massy *Swynnerton* (1877-1938), an English-born entomologist, born in India and worked in Eastern Africa; he wrote *On the birds of Gazaland, Southern Rhodesia;* he was killed in an air- crash (Beolens & Watkins, 2003, pp. 332) (swynnertoni, swynnerton's robin, 312, 925) G. E. Shelley, 1906.

sylvaticus L. inhabitant of or pertaining to the woods; *silva silvae* wood, forest, plantation, shrubbery; (bradypterus, knysna warbler, 316, 793, C. J. Sundevall, 1858) (turnix, kurrichane buttonquail, 132, 118, R. L. Desfontaines, 1787).

sylvia L. a warbler, inhabitant of or pertaining to the woods; *silva silvae* wood, forest, plantation, shrubbery (51).

sylvietta L. a warbler, inhabitant of or pertaining to the woods; diminutive of *sylvia; silva silvae* wood, forest, plantation, shrubbery (51).

symonsi after Roden E. *Symons* (1884-1972), collector and game conservator, mainly in KwaZulu Natal; the common name of the bird refers to the 1000 km long mountain range that takes its name from Afrikaans and it means 'dragon mountains' (crithagra, drakensberg siskin, 410, 1132) Roberts, 1916.

T

tachiro French; *la tache* a spot or blotch; *rond* round, referring to the rufous and brown blotched underparts (accipiter, african goshawk, 108, 512) F. M. Daudin 1800.

tachybaptus Gr. fast diver; *tachys (ταχύς)* fast, swift; baptes *(βάπτης)* diver, dipper; *bapto (βάπτω)* to dip, to sink, to dive, to dip in dye; priests of Cotytto, goddess of sex in Thrace, were called *baptes (βάπτες)* because they used to dip their hair in water during their obscene ceremonies during the night; Eng. *bapt*ize, *bapt*ism; (41).

tachymarptis Gr. fast snatcher; *tachys (ταχύς)* fast, swift; *marptis,-ios (μάρπτις, -ιος)* he who seizes, grabs, snatches; *marpto (μάρπτω)* to seize, to grab, to snatch (32).

tadorna from Celtic roots *tadorna* pied waterfowl and French *tadorne* Common Shelduck (27).

tahapisi probably from Tswana; Jobling suggests *thagapitse* or *thaxapitsi* zebra bird, for various stripe-headed finches and weavers (2010, pp. 378) (emberiza, cinnamon-breasted bunting, 412, 1134) A. Smith, 1836.

talatala Tswana very green; *tala* green (cinnyris, white-bellied sunbird, 374 993) A. Smith, 1836.

tauraco *English name Touraco coined by Edwards (1743), based on a supposed West African native name* (Jobling, 2010, pp. 380) (32).

tchagra onomatopoeic for the bird's grating call by Levaillant (Robert's 2009, 48) (tchagra,

southern tchagra, 360, 694) L. J. P. Vieillot, 1819.

telacanthura Gr. tail with spiny tip; *telos (τέλος)* completion, end; *akantha (ἄκανθα)* thorn, fish spine, a thorny plant; *oura* (οὐρά) tail (32).

telophorus Gr. to carry far, referring to loud ringing calls of Bokmakierie (Roberts, 2009, pp. 48); *telos (τέλος)* completion, end; *fero (φέρω)* to carry, to bring; *-foros (-φόρος)* he who carries or brings (32).

temminckii after Coenraad Jacob *Temminck* (1778-1858), a rich Dutch collector, ornithologist and illustrator, first Director of the Leiden Rijksmuseum van Naturlijke Historie from 1820 to 1858; he wrote *Manuel d'ornithologie, ou tableau Systematique des Oiseaux qui se trouvent en Europe* and *Nouveau Recueil de Planches Coloriees d'Oiseaux* (calidris, temminck's stint, 164, 368, J. P. A. Leisler, 1812) (cursorius, temminck's courser, 180, 426, W. J. Swainson, 1822).

tenellus L. delicate; *tenellus* very delicate, very tender; *tener* tender, soft, gentle, weak, frail, young, immature (tmetothylacus, golden pipit, 356, 1097) J. Cabanis, 1878.

tenuirostris L. slender-billed; *tenuis* thin, delicate, weak, slender; *rostrum* bill (anous, lesser noddy, 196, 473. C. J. Temminck, 1823.) (calidris, great knot, 162, 364, T. Horsfield, 1821).

terathopius Gr. marvel appearance; *teras, teratos (τέρας, τέρατος)* monster, marvel, wonder, meteor; *ops, opos (ὤψ, ὀπός)* appearance, eye, face; <u>Tera</u>byte=the fourth power of 1000 or 10¹² or 1000 *Giga*bytes (40).

terpsiphone Gr. delightful voice; *terpsis (τέρψις)* delight, pleasure; *terpo (τέρπω)* to please; phone *(φωνή)* voice; Eng. tele<u>phone</u>, <u>phone</u>tics, gramo<u>phone</u> (47).

terrestris L. terrestrial; *terrestris* by or on land, terrestrial, of the farm; *terra* earth, land, ground, country, region; Eng. <u>terra</u>ce, Medi<u>terra</u>nean=Middle Earth (phyllastrephus, terrestrial brownbul, 294, 774) W. J. Swainson, 1837.

textrix L. female weaver; *textrix* female weaver, the Fates; *texere* to weave, construct with care,

plait (cisticola, cloud cicticola, 330, 840) L. J. P. Vieillot, 1817.

thalassarche Gr. ruler of the sea; *thalassa (θάλασσα)* sea; *arche (ἀρχή)* power, command, beginning (45).

thalassoica Gr. sea-dweller; *thalassa (θάλασσα)* sea; *oicos* or *ecos (οἶκος)* house, habitat; *oikeo (οἰκέω)* to inhabit, to reside; Eng. <u>eco</u>logy, <u>eco</u>nomy (46).

thalassornis Gr. sea bird; *thalassa (θάλασσα)* sea; *ornis (ὄρνις)* bird; the word for bird was both male and female in ancient Gr.; in modern Gr. it is female and it means chicken (26).

thamnolaea Gr. bush thrush; *thamnos (θάμνος)* bush; *laios (λαιός)* thrush probably *turdus torquatus* (55).

thomensis after Sao Tomé, one of the two main islands of Sao Tomé & Principe, the second smallest country in Africa and the smallest Portuguese-speaking country in the world (estrilda, cinderella waxbill, 396, 1050) J. A. de Sousa, 1888.

thoracica Gr. of the chest, pectoral; *thorax, thoracos (θώραξ, θώρακος)* chest, breastplate (usually made of copper) (apalis, bar-throated apalis, 326, 850) G. Shaw, 1811.

threskiornis Gr. religious or sacred bird; *threskeia (θρησκεία)* religion, religious worship; *ornis (ὄρνις)* bird; the sacred ibis was venerated in Ancient Egypt as a symbol of the god Thoth, who was depicted as a man with the head of an ibis or a baboon; his role was to maintain the universe, being on one side of Ra's boat and his wife Ma'at on the other and later he was associated with arbitration on godly disputes, art of magic etc; according to one explanation Thoth's Egyptian name *dhwty* is the oldest name for the ibis (43).

thula Jobling (2010, pp. 385) reports that this was the Araucano name for another bird (black-necked swan *cygnus melanocryphus*) and was erroneously given to the snowy egret by Molina (egretta, snowy egret, 64, 587) J. I. Molina, 1782.

tinniens L. ringing, tinkling; *tinnire* ring, clang, utter a shrill/metallic sound (cisticola, levaillant's cisticola, 334, 834) M. Lichtenstein, 1842.

tmetothylacus Gr. separate pouch; Roberts speculates it refers to '*bare lower tibia, unusual among passerines*'; *tmetos (τμητός)* cut, shape by cutting; *temno (τέμνω)* intersect, cut; *thylakos (θύλακος)* sac, pocket; from the word to cut in Gr. comes the word a<u>tom</u>; it means uncut or cannot be cut any more (59).

tockus Jobling (2010, pp. 387) reports that French name 'Tock' was given to two hornbills by de Buffon (1770-1783) said to be based on an onomatopoeic Senegalese name (29).

torquatus L. collared, adorned with a necklace; *torques* collar, necklace, neckchain; *torquere* to turn, to twist, to bend (lanioturdus, white-tailed shrike, 364, 712, G. R. Waterhouse, 1838) (lybius, black-collared barbet, 252, 146, C. Dumont de Sainte Croix, 1816) (saxicola, african stonechat, 304, 946, C. Linnaeus, 1766).

totanus from Italian name *Totano* for the common redshank; L. *totus, tota, totum* whole, all, entire, complete; *-an, -anus* suffix that indicates former gens (tringa, common redshank, 166, 352) C. Linnaeus, 1758.

totta from Hottentot (Khoikhoi) peoples of South Africa; Hottentot is the former name for the indigenous Khoi Khoi people of southern Africa; Dutch settlers named them Hottentots, immitating the sound of their language; today the term is considered derogatory (crithagra, cape siskin, 410, 1131) A. E. Sparrman, 1786.

tracheliotos Gr. trachelia *(τραχήλια)* parts of meat and cartilage around the neck that was usually thrown away; ous, otos *(οὖς, ὠτός)* ear, gristly ears; it refers to the wattles of the bird; Eng. *oto*rinolaryngologist (aegypius, lappet-faced vulture, 86, 491) J.R. Forster, 1796.

trachyphonus Gr. harsh-voiced; *trachys, -eos (τραχύς,-εος)* rough, harsh, throaty; *phone (φωνή)* voice; Eng. tele*phone*, *phone*tics, gramo*phone* (28).

tractrac onomatopoeic name from Levaillant's *le Traquet* (wheatear) in 1805 (cercomela, tractrac chat, 302, 954) Wilkes, 1817.

treron Gr. trembling, shy, timid; *treron,-onos (τρήρων,-ωνος)* shy, timid, easily alarmed; *treo (τρέω)* flee because of fear,

fear something; a word known since Homer's time and usually attributed to wild pigeons (34).

tricholaema Gr. hairy throat; *thrix, trihos (θρίξ, τριχός)* hair; *triha (τρίχα)* in modern Gr.; *laemos (λαιμός)* throat (28).

tricollaris L. three collared; *tri* three; *collare, -ris* collar (charadrius, three-banded plover, 152, 400) L. J. P. Vieillot, 1818.

tricolor L. three colours; *tri* three; *color, coloris* colour, complexion, beauty, lustre (pycnonotus, dark-capped bulbul, 294, 766, G. Hartlaub, 1862) (steganopus, wilson's phalarope, 174, 378, L. J. P. Vieillot, 1819).

tridactyla Gr. three-toed; *tria (τρία)* three; *dactylos (δάκτυλος)* finger, toe (rissa, black-legged kittiwake, 184, 449) C. Linnaeus, 1758.

tringa Gr. sandpiper; *trungas (τρύγγας)* was an unidendified bird mentioned by Aristotle, a pygargos, rump shaking; probably *totanus ochropus* (36).

tristigma Gr. three marks, stigmata; *tria (τρία)* three; *stigma (στίγμα)* stigma, mark; *stizo (στίζω)* to mark with a blunt tool (caprimulgus, freckled nightjar, 226, 266) E. Rüppell, 1840.

tristis L. sad, gloomy or dull coloured; *tristis* sad, sorrowful, gloomy (acridotheres, common myna, 370, 972) C. Linnaeus, 1766. Myna is from the Hindi word मैना (maina) starling.

trivialis L. common; *trivialis* common, ordinary; *trivium* crossroads, public street, where three roads intersect (anthus, tree pipit, 354, 1113) C. Linnaeus, 1758.

trizonatus Gr. three-banded; *tria (τρία)* three; *zone (ζώνη)* girdle, belt (buteo, forest buzzard, 102, 523) Rudebeck, 1957.

trochilus Gr. a bird mentioned by Herodotus and described to take leeches from the mouth of crocodiles; it wasn't leeches but mosquitoes and it is the *charadrius aegyptiacus*; Aristotle uses the same name for the *troglodytes europaeus* also called *king* or *ambassador* (phylloscopus, willow warbler, 314, 807) C. Linnaeus, 1758.

trochocercus Gr. round tail, with reference to fanning tail; *trochos (τροχός)* he who runs, anything round, wheel, disc; *trecho (τρέχω)* to run; *cercos (κέρκος)* animal tail (47).

tropica Gr. of the tropics; *tropikos (τροπικός)* tropical; related to the solstice, an astronomical event that occurs twice each year as the Sun reaches its highest or lowest point relative to the celestial equator on the celestial sphere (fregetta, black-bellied storm-petrel, 46, 636) J. Gould, 1844.

trygnites Gr. resembling a sandpiper; *trungas (τρύγγας)* was an unidendified bird mentioned by Aristotle, a pygargos, rump shaking; probably *totanus ochropus* (36).

turdoides L. & Gr. thrush-like; L. *turdus* thrush; Gr. *-oides (-οειδές)* resembling (51).

turdus L. thrush; *turdus* thrush (56).

turnix L. quail; *coturnix, -icis* quail; abbreviation from *coturnix* quail, to show the resemblance to quails (27).

turtur L. turtle-dove; *turtur, -ris* turtle-dove (pachyptila, fairy prion, 34, 666, H. Kuhl, 1820) (streptopelia, european turtle-dove, 202, 281, C. Linnaeus, 1758).

tympanistria Gr. female drummer; *tympanistria (τυμπανίστρια)* female drummer; *tympanon (τύμπανον)* drum; the *tympanon* drum was associated to the ceremonies in honour of Cybele and Dionysus and according to one hypothesis the word is a loan from Semitic languages (Hebrew *top* pl. *tuppim*, Aramaic *tuppa*) (turtur, tambourine dove, 132, 288, C. J. Temminck, 1810).

typus L. type; *typus* type, figure, pattern, prototype, model, symbol (polyboroides, african harrier-hawk, 100, 505) A. Smith, 1829.

tyto Gr. night-owl; *tyto (τυτώ)* night owl (32).

U

umbretta It derives either from *umber* and refers to the colour of the bird (a uniform brown colour) or from L. *umbra, -ae*, shadow, shade, darkness, night, ghost and also cover, protection; *umbrare* to cast a shadow; common name refers to the shape of the head (scopus, hamerkop, 74, 603) J. F. Gmelin, 1789.

undulata L. wavy or wave-like; *unda* wave, sea, smoke swirl; *undula* small wave; *undare* to make waves; referring to "patterning of breast feathers"(Roberts, 2009) (anas, yellow-billed duck, 82,107) C.F. Dubois, 1837.

upupa L. hoopoe; onomatopoeic for call, as is hoopoe (29).

uraeginthus Gr. sparrow-tailed; oura *(oὐρά)* tail; *aiginthus* or *aegithus (αἴγινθος or αἴγιθος)* sparrow (58).

urbicum L. from the city or frequenting towns; *urbicus* or *urbanus* of the city, funny, educated, elegant; *urbs, urbis* town (city, mainly Rome) (delichon, common house-martin, 280, 762) C. linnaeus, 1758.

urinatrix L. diver; *urinare* dive, plunge in the water; *urinator* diver, swimmer (pelecanoides, common diving-petrel, 48, 1142) J. F. Gmelin, 1789.

urocolius Gr. scabbard- tailed; referring to long tail; oura (oὐρά) tail; *koloios (κόλοιος)* jackdaw, jay, magpie or *koleos (κολεός)* scabbard, sheath with reference to the long tail.

ussheri after Herbert Taylor *Ussher* (1836-1880), who collected the type specimen; he was a British civil servant and Governor of Tobago, probably Labuan, Borneo and later of the Gold Coast (telacanthura, mottled spinetail, 230, 231) R. B. Sharpe, 1870.

usticollis L. burnt-necked; *ustus* burnt; *urere* to burn or to scorch; *collum,-i* neck (eremomela, burnt-necked eremomela, 324, 789) C. J. Sundevall, 1850.

V

vaalensis from the Vaal river; the largest tributary to the Orange river; in Dutch and Afrikaans it means 'drab' or 'dull' and has to do with the colour of the water, especially during the floods; the early KhoiKhoi name of the river was 'Tky' and it also meant drab or dull; other local names of the upper parts of the river refer to the mountains in the area namely *Likwa, Ikwa, Ilikwa, Lekwa* etc. (anthus, buffy pipit, 352, 1107) G. E. Shelley, 1900.

vaillantii after Francois *Levaillant* or Le *Vaillant* (1753-1824), French traveller, author, ornithologist and explorer; a pioneer in many ways Levaillant was among the first to use coloured plates of birds; he opposed Linnaeus' binomial nomenclature and gave French names to birds (trachyphonus, crested barbet, 252, 147) C. Ranzani, 1821.

vanellus L. lapwing; *'named for its floppy wing action resembling a winnowing fan (vannus) or the sound their wings make when they fly'* (Roberts, 2005); *vannus* sieve; *vanus* thin, empty, vain, idle, false, cheat, arrogant (37).

variegatus L. variegated, exhibiting different colours, irregularly marked; refers to the scaly throat; *varius* various, variegated, multicoloured (indicator, scaly-throated honeyguide, 250, 122) R-P. Lesson, 1830.

velatus L. masked, covered or concealed; *velare* to cover, to conceal, to hide; *velum* screen, curtain (ploceus, southern masked-weaver, 384, 1016) L. J. P. Vieillot, 1819.

venustus L. charming, attractive, beautiful, gaceful; *venus* beauty, grace; Venus is the name of the Roman goddess of love, beauty, fertility, and sex; her

Gr. counterpart *Aphrodite* gets her name, according to one etymology from aphros (ἀφρός) foam as it was said that she was born from sea foam (cinnyris, variable sunbird, 374, 992) G. Shaw, 1799.

vermiculatus L. marked with sinuous or wavy lines, mosaic, vermiculated; *vermis* worm; *vermiculus* grub, larva, little worm (burhinus, water thick-knee, 178, 386) J. L. Cabanis, 1868.

veroxii/verreauxii after Jean Baptiste Edouard *Verreaux* (1810-1868) and his brother Jules Pierre (1807-1873), French naturalists, collectors and dealers who worked at the Cape, nephews of Delalande (aquila, verreaux's or black eagle, 96, 531, R-P. Lesson 1830) (cyanomitra, grey sunbird, 378, 980, A. Smith, 1831).

verticalis L. crowned, of the head; *vertex, verticis* crown of the head, top, peak, edge, whirl; also vertical, perpendicular, upright (eremopterix, grey-backed sparrowlark, 272, 888) A. Smith, 1836.

vespertinus L. of evening, of twilight; *vesper,-eris* evening

star, evening, west; related to Gr. *hesperos (ἕσπερος)* west, evening star, the planet Venus (falco, red-footed falcon, 122, 551) C. Linnaeus, 1766.

vetula L. old woman; *vetulus, a, um* somewhat old; diminutive of *vetus,-eris* old, ancient, experienced; larus dominicanus vetula is the subspecies that can be found in southern Africa; although it is quite different from the other subspecies it is not treated as a distinct species (larus dominicanus, 188, 439) M. Lichtenstein, 1823.

vexillarius L. standard-bearer; *vexillum* flag, banner; *veho* to bear, to carry; Eng. vehicle; *velum* curtain, screen (macrodipteryx, pennant-winged nightjar, 226, 274) J. Gould, 1838.

victorini after Johan Fredrick *Victorin* (1831-1855), a Swedish traveller who visited the Cape Colony and died there of tuberculosis in 1855; he wrote *Journey to the Cape Land in the years 1853-1855* and also *Hunting and Nature Scenes* (cryptillas, victorin's warbler, 316, 783) C. J. Sundevall, 1860.

vidua L. widow, referring to black plumage or widow's train (long tail of some species); *viduus, a, um* widower, deserted, bereaved; *viduare* to bereave, to devastate (58)

viduata L. widowed; *viduus, a, um* widower, deserted, bereaved; *viduare* to bereave, to devastate (dendrocygna, white-faced duck, 80, 85) C. Linnaeus, 1766.

vigorsii after Nicholas Aylward *Vigors* (1785-1840), an Irish zoologist and politician; co-founder of the Zoological Society of London and its first Secretary and also founder of the predecessor of the Royal Entomological Society of London; he described many birds and wrote plenty of papers on Ornithology (eupodotis, karoo korhaan, 148, 301) A. Smith, 1831.

vinaceigula L. red wine-coloured throat; *vinaceus* vinaceous, of grapes; *vinum* wine Eng. wine, Fr. vin, Ger. Wein; *gula* throat, gullet (egretta, slaty egret, 66, 581) R. B. Sharpe, 1895.

violacea L. violet-coloured; *violaceus, a, um* violet-coloured, of a purplish-blue colour; (anthobaphes, orange-breasted

sunbird, 372, 977) C. Linnaeus, 1766.

virens L. green; *vireo* to be green, to be fresh, flourish (zosterops, cape white-eye, 344, 822) C. J. Sundevall, 1850.

virgata L. streaked, striped; *virga, ae* staff, green branch; *vireo* to be green, to be fresh, flourish; the common name of the bird is after the Kerguelen islands, one of the most desolate places on earth, in the south Indian Ocean, discovered by Yves-Joseph de *Kerguelen*-Trémarec, a French navigator, in 1772 (sterna, kerguelen tern, 192) J. Cabanis, 1875.

viridis L. green; *vireo* to be green, to be fresh, flourish (telophorus, gorgeous bush-shrike, 362, 705, L. J. P. Vieillot, 1817) (terpsiphone, african paradise-flycatcher, 342, 686, P. L. Statius Müller, 1776).

vittata L. banded, ornamented with bands; *vitta,- ae* band, ribbon, strip; in the case of the prion it refers to the M on the wings and in the case of the tern to white facial streak (pachyptila, broad-billed prion, 34, 663, G. Forster, 1777) (sterna, antarctic tern, 192, 461, J. F. Gmelin, 1789).

vocifer L. vociferous; *vox, vocis* voice, sound, cry, call, language; *fero* to carry, bring; Gr. fero *(φέρω)* bring, carry; Eng. vociferate; the bird is called *hungwe* in Shona and i*nkwazi* in isiZulu (haliaeetus, african fish eagle, 90, 481) F. M. Daudin, 1800.

vulgaris L. common; *vulgaris* usual, common, everyday, vulgar; *vulgus* people, common people, crowd, vulgar people; Eng. folk, Ger. Volk (sturnus, common starling, 370, 971) C. Linnaeus, 1758.

vulpinus L. fox-like; *vulpes, vulpis* fox, cunning, sly; the rufous form of the bird has a colour similar to that of a fox (buteo, steppe buzzard, 102, 522) C. W. L. Gloger, 1833.

W

wahlbergi after Johan August *Wahlberg* (1810-1856), a Swedish naturalist and collector; he travelled and collected in southern Africa until his untimely death by a wounded elephant (aquila, wahlberg's eagle, 100, 536) C. J. Sundevall, 1851.

whytii after Alexander *Whyte* FLS (1834-1905), a governement naturalist in Nyasaland (now Malawi), where he collected extensively under the patronage of Sir Harry Johnston (Beolens & Watkins, 2003, pp.366) (stactolaema, whyte's barbet, 252, 139, G.E. Shelley, 1893) (sylvietta, red-faced crombec, 328, 784 G. E. Shelley, 1894).

wilkinsi after Captain Sir George Hubert *Wilkins* (1888-1958), an Australian polar explorer and ornithologist; he was much more than that though; there are reports that he was a war correspondent, polar explorer, naturalist, geographer, climatologist, aviator, author, balloonist, war hero, reporter, secret agent, submariner and navigator! (Beolens & Watkins, 2003, pp.367); he explored both the Arctic and the Antarctic (nesospiza, wilkins' bunting, 414) P. R. Lowe, 1903.

woodfordii after Colonel E. J. A. *Woodford* (1761-1835), an early collector and British officer, reported to have fought in Salamanca in 1812 and Waterloo in 1815 (strix, african wood-owl, 220, 260) A. Smith, 1834.

X

Z

xanthops blonde or golden faced or eyed; *xanthos (ξανθός)* blonde, wheat gold, ops *(ὤψ)* face or eye (ploceus, golden weaver, 386, 1014) G. Hartlaub & Finsch, 1862.

xanthopterus blonde or golden winged; *xanthos (ξανθός)* blonde, wheat gold, pteron *(πτερόν)* wing (ploceus, southern brown-throated weaver, 386, 1015) Hartlaub & Finsch, 1870.

xema Jobling reports two or three versions; Gr. xene *(ξένη)*, stranger, foreign (1991) or that it is one of randomly coined words because authors had difficulty finding names that had never been used before (2009); a third explanation is Gr. xeme *(χήμη)* which means chasm or a type of sea shell (not yawning); we think more probable from Gr. *exemeo (ἐξεμέω)* to vomit, to throw up (sabini, sabine's gull, 186) J. Sabine, 1819.

xenus Gr. stranger, foreign; xenos *(ξένος)* strange, foreign, alien, unfamiliar, unknown; Eng. *xeno*-phobia *(ξενοφοβία)* fear of strangers or something foreign (36).

zambesiae after Zambezi, the fourth longest river in Africa, the largest flowing in the Indian ocean; the name of the river is disputed; according to some it derives from the M'biza or Bisa people, of central-eastern Zambia or 'mbeze', a Bantu term for 'river of fish'; David Livingstone's record is quite interesting as he suggests different names from tribes that live along the river and they all mean 'large river'; Luambeji, Luambesi, Ambezi, Ojimbesi and Zambesi (prodotiscus, green-backed honeybird, 250, 126) G. E. Shelley, 1894.

zeylonus from Ceylon; C. Linnaeus was led to believe that the species came from there; Ceylon is the old name of modern day Sri Lanka; Ceilao was the name given to the island by the Portuguese in 1505 and it was anglicised as Ceylon (telophorus, bokmakierie, 362, 700) C. Linnaeus, 1766.

zoothera Gr. animal hunter; zoo *(ζῶο)* animal; *thera (θήρα) hunting wild animals; therao (θηράω)* to hunt wild animals; refers to arthropod diet

(Roberts, 2005); the Greek word for hunting is also in the scientific names of lion, leopard etc (pan-*thera*) and the common name of pan-*ther*; it means 'hunter of everything'; animal in Gr. derives from zoe *(ζωή)* life; in English it derives from *anima* spirit, soul, mind, air ie having breath; L. *animal, -lis* animal (54).

zosterops Gr. girdle or belt and eye, referring to rings around the eyes; *zoster (ζωστήρ)* belt or girdle;ops *(ὤψ)* eye (52).

Bibliography

Robert's Birds of Southern Africa, Hockey, Dean & Ryan, VII edition, 2009.

Helm Dictionary of scientific Bird names, J. A. Jobling, 2010, London.

Whose bird? Beolens & Watkins, 2003

Complete photographic field guide, Birds of Southern Africa, Sinclair & Ryan, SASOL, Struik Nature, 2009.

Collins Latin Dictionary & Grammar, 1st edition, 1997.

Etymological and translation Dictionary of Latin, V. A. Kouvelas, Macedonian editions, 2002, Athens.

Dictionary of modern Greek, G. Babiniotis, Lexicology centre, 1998, Athens.

Etymological Dictionary of modern Greek, G. Babiniotis, Lexicology centre, 2010, Athens.

In the land of Myth, D. & L. del Corno, Livanis, Athens, 2004.

Dictionary of Ancient Greek, Lyddell, Scott, Sideris, Athens, 1984.